NICK OF TIME

MY LIFE AND CAREER,
ALL ON THE RECORD

NICK OF TIME

MY LIFE AND CAREER,
ALL ON THE RECORD

BY NICK HAMPTON

ORiGiN™ IMPRiNT

First published in Australia in 2020
by ORiGiN™ IMPRiNT
ABN 46 111 477 895
originimprint.com

 A catalogue record for this book is available from the National Library of Australia

Hampton, Nick, author.
Nick of Time
ISBN: 978-0-6485874-5-3

Cover design by Andrew Mortlock
Art Direction by Philip Mortlock
Editing by Gary Martin
Typeset by Amber Quin

ORiGiN™ IMPRiNT
PO Box 1235
QVB Post Office
NSW 1230 Australia
originimprint.com

THE TOP TEN

Nick's colourful description of life in the music industry brought back a flood of memories. Reflections that mirrored some of my views regarding the mega-egos and bad decisions makers, but more importantly highlighted the extraordinary visionaries and talented ones. His journey has been long and varied and his achievements many. Thank you for a good read!

Fifa Riccobono – Former CEO of Albert Music

Thanks to too many years at the wild and woolly end of the rock 'n' roll industry, followed by even more years in business dealing with the advertising industry, I've developed Pistanthrophobia. It's nothing to do with excessive alcohol consumption (well not entirely), it is the inability to trust other people. So imagine my surprise when I met Nick Hampton those many decades ago. Could it be possible that the big smile before me was genuine? Was Nick's desire to help others less fortunate a ruse for some other agenda? Could he really have this much care and concern and yet be pragmatic enough with a "let's just do this" attitude to effect real change? You bet! Trust is rarer than diamonds in this industry but Nick is a trust billionaire. And he spends this trust very wisely by corralling the world-weary cynics in our industry together for purpose. There are a lot of well meaning do-gooders who can just talk the talk. Few are the Nick Hampton kind. I still suffer from Pistanthrophobia. But I put this down to there being too few Nick Hamptons in this world.

Les Gock – Founding member of Hush and
legendary advertising jingle executive

I had such a good time this weekend reading Nick's book. Congratulations, it's a lovely read for someone who has known some of his life but not all. Whoever said chartered accountants were boring has never met Nick Hampton. From pre-war London through Paris, New York, Australia and then finally back to France, what an interesting journey. The details and the characters that he has met along the way make for a wonderful read. I could not put it down!

Peter Rix – Manager of Marcia Hines, Jon English,
event maestro and entrepreneur

Memories: the mental capacity or faculty of retaining and reviving facts, events, impressions, etcetera. *Nick of Time* brought back memories in spades in this great read highlighting the characters and his experiences during the glory days of the global music industry. It certainly lit up the corners of my mind. I read it in a single sitting, and I am sure that many others will find it equally as interesting. Well done, Nick, congratulations.

Bob Aird – Former music industry executive

In my roles as managing director of Mushroom Music and a board member of APRA and AMCOS I knew Nick as the affable and very competent APRA company secretary for many years, helping Brett Cottle keep the ship on course. He brought a calm confidence to what could sometimes be a combative environment when the broadcasters, record labels or concert promoters decided to arc up. Those achievements in themselves would constitute a well fulfilled career. Then I started reading this book. I had no idea of the breadth of his experiences and the more than colourful characters he worked with. If you wanted to describe a dream career you might as well start in the record business with a job in London in 1964 with Pye Records. They had a new band from Muswell Hill called The Kinks and three of the greatest songs that are still played to this day – *You Really Got Me, Waterloo*

Sunset and *Sunny Afternoon*. Then onto the rollercoaster – Paris, America, England, in several quite different roles, and finally managing EMI Records in Sydney. The refreshing thing is that Nick doesn't just do a roll call of famous artists and music executives. He comments on their character in some detail. Not all of it is sweet. When some people deserve to be called out he does it deftly and with precision. There is often comedy in those caricatures. To end gracefully, Nick and Jenny Morris did wonderful work for the Nordoff-Robbins music therapy charity. Arise, Sir Nick, we're very fortunate you found your way to Australia and graced us for so long.

Ian James – Former MD of Mushroom Music

Find debonair in the dictionary and the description is as follows: Nick Hampton. Nick is of course so much more than just debonair. I have observed his skills in strategy, diplomacy, forward thinking, numbers, logistics and outcomes. Brains AND beauty! I will be forever grateful to him for introducing me to the world of Nordoff-Robbins music therapy, but I love him most because he cares . . . about people, places and things.

**Jenny Morris OAM, MNZM – Chair APRA,
Director Nordoff-Robbins Music Therapy Australia**

In the simplest of terms Nordoff-Robbins Music Therapy Australia may not exist without Nick's commitment, vision, passion and perseverance. Nick should be proud to have positively changed the lives of tens of thousands of people with disabilities and other challenges. Although there is now some physical distance between us, Nick will always remain "Mr Nordoff-Robbins".

**Simon Thorp – Chair Nordoff-Robbins Music
Therapy Australia**

Nick Hampton was the key to two major life-changing events for me. In 1995 after a short time dabbling in artist management, Nick had the final say (after three interviews) in appointing me to the very sought after membership position with APRA AMCOS as a junior representative. Twenty-five years later I am still there and loving it more each day. Gently and ever so persuasively he introduced me to the world of music therapy and insisted that my skill set would be crucial for the board of Nordoff-Robbins, which led to my appointment in 2008. To this day I remain in both these roles, which has ultimately changed the course of my life, and for that I am forever grateful to Nick Hampton. Thank you.

Milly Petriella – Director of Member Relations, APRA AMCOS

Why is it always those quiet accounting types who remember where the bodies were buried? Nick has written a real page-turner which gives a real overview of the music industry over seven decades. The man has a memory like an elephant!

Norm Lurie – Retired MD of Music Sales Australia

Nick Hampton – charming and honourable. A gentleman but with a steely core. Not someone to be trifled with!

Jeremy Fabinyi – Manager and retired music industry executive

My conversations with Nick have always been sparkling – full of his knowledge and charm. The memoir lets us know just how he became the charismatic and hugely effective person we all know in Australia and reveals a lot we didn't know about the trials and fun he went through to become so respected and revered.

Iva Davies – Australian singer, songwriter, multi-instrumentalist and Icehouse founder

Nick is a larger than life personality with enthusiasms covering many differing areas. The one that captured Slim's attention and mine was his ambition to establish a Nordoff-Robbins facility in Sydney for those people whose intellectual disabilities interfered with their access to music and its enjoyment, but who often responded to playing and hearing music. Through meeting one such young girl on our first tour of Victoria's Gippsland, we became part of the amazing change music made in Allison. She was unable to speak and made no effort to, up until the age of about eight or nine when she heard Slim singing on the radio. Ally began listening intently and trying to follow the words. The family bought her a gramophone and Slim records. Allison began to try singing along with Slim. Over the years, from that start, music of all kinds became her outlet and love. It was her contact with the world, and from there she began to reach out to life around her.

We saw that happen over many years. Nick's efforts brought big changes into families such as Allison's. No wonder Slim and I became ambassadors and supporters of the Nordoff-Robbins venture!

Joy McKean – Legendary Australian country music singer-songwriter and wife of the late Slim Dusty

CONTENTS

THANKS

Let me begin by saying thanks to all these people.

From those early days at Eastbourne: Nigel Mundy and John Raeburn. We've always kept in touch, just.

From the Sixties: the late Jack Gill, Louis Benjamin, Les Cocks and all the Friday evening crowd from The Mason's Arms; Terry Stanley. Not too many of us left now.

From EMI: the late Clive May and Tony Todman, Jochen Frese and the late Wilf Jung.

From APRA: Brett Cottle, Dean Ormston, Gus Jansen, Kathryn Williams and Jennifer Reynolds.

From NRMTA: the late Robin Howat, Iani Sujono, Rob Devlin and board members Judith Rutherford, Jenny Morris, Les Gock, David Albert, Simon Thorp, Cameron Slapp and Chris Gardoll.

Good friends: David Mellor, Terry and the late Kerrie Gray, Alex and Gloria Coroneos, Fifa Riccobono, Tracey Meredith and Paul Marx, Anne and Ian Smith.

The team who have taken this book from dream to reality: publisher and friend Philip Walker and Kwan, and editor extraordinary Gary Martin. Many thanks to Philip Mortlock, Amber Quin, Nick Young and everyone at Origin.

And not to forget the family: Valerie who is still a friend after sixty years, Jean with whom I am still enjoying a very happy life, my three great children, Juliet, Jerry and Lucy, and the seven grandchildren: Charlotte (Charlie), Will, Jemima, Jessie, Daisy, Sebastian and Isobel. I am so proud of you all and happy to still be part of a group that enjoys getting together.

'The advantage of a bad memory
is that one enjoys several times
the same good things for the first time.'

Friedrich Nietzsche

PREFACE

Typically boring, definitely not cool, mild-mannered accountant just happens to be in the right place at the right time to get a start in the amazing world of rock 'n' roll and make international record labels his home for more than two decades.

Sounds like an unlikely outline for a really riveting piece of pulp fiction, doesn't it? *The Musical Adventures of a Quiet Bean Counter*. Except that it's not fiction, it's true, and I'm the bean counter, though perhaps not your usual one. And so this is my story, and my life.

My career in the music industry started in London, took me all over Europe, to America, Australia and New Zealand, and gave me executive jobs with giant labels like EMI and CBS, as well as some smaller ones that punched way above their weight when it came to hits and hit-makers.

I would hate to be remembered only as a name-dropper, but the fact is my time in music, behind the scenes, brought me into contact with dozens of artists, movers and assorted shakers who I think everyone in the business has heard of. The list, in no particular order, includes Petula Clark, Tony Hatch, Jackie Trent, The Kinks, Donovan, Dick James, Elton John, Sandie Shaw, Johnny Cash, Andy Williams, Tony Bennett, Vera Lynn, Lew Grade and Clive Davis. And from my time in Sydney, Slim Dusty and Joy McKean, Ted Albert, Glenn Shorrock, Smoky Dawson, Jenny Morris, Jimmy Barnes, Iva Davies, Neil Finn and Richard Clapton, to name just a few, not to mention the wonderfully large cast of fine people I got to know through APRA, AMCOS and then through Nordoff-Robbins, the world of music therapy.

I ended up spending forty years in the music business, seeing mostly the good, occasionally the bad, and sometimes the downright ugly. In writing this memoir, I decided to dive in where it all began, London in the early sixties. This will take me up to my arrival in Australia for my period as managing director of EMI in the eighties. Then I'll tell you a bit about my ancestors and the world this very middle-class boy grew up in, before I return to Oz for my post-EMI days and round it all off.

I hope you enjoy the read, because I certainly enjoyed the ride.

NICK HAMPTON
Castres, France
April 2020

SECTION ONE:
A START AND
A PART IN SHOWBIZ

1. Enter via ATV

IT'S funny how things sometimes pan out in life.

I unwittingly got into the record business through television after landing a job at ATV in 1962. Associated Television Limited had won the licences to broadcast in London on the weekends and Birmingham during the week, back in 1956. After early losses – when most homes could only receive the BBC television service – ATV started to make money. Lots. The initial revenue projections were beaten out of sight. As an example, the director of sales was rewarded by a commission scheme which earned him enough to have his own Rolls-Royce and employ a personal chauffeur. The company garage was full of Rollers and Bentleys, and the programming director had an Aston Martin. Little wonder that Lew Grade, the deputy managing director, was credited as saying a commercial television station "was a licence to print money", although that quote was also attributed to Lord Thomson of Scottish TV.

By the time I arrived at the ATV complex in Great Cumberland Place in the heart of London, all the employees were enjoying an annual bonus of twenty per cent and pay increases were generous. Members of the ETU (Electrical Trades Union) at the studios were among the best paid tradesmen in the country, but that did not stop them holding the company to ransom from time to time: no electricians equals no broadcast.

The profits were being heavily invested in other "entertainment" businesses. ITC, Lew Grade's film production company, was one of the first, and ATV also had interests in commercial radio and television stations in Canada and Australia, as well as the British licence for Muzak (famously known as "lift music") and Ambassador Bowling, which was opening tenpin alleys all over the UK.

By 1962, the group financial controller, Jack Gill, was having difficulty in compiling all the investment information and reporting regularly to his board, as well as overseeing a large accounting function. I was brought in as Jack's first assistant.

My principal job was to review all the incoming financial reports, chase up laggards, and draft updates on each arm of investment for Jack to present at the monthly board meetings. This could have been boring anywhere else but not at ATV, where there was always either a celebration or a crisis, often both on the same day.

The board members included Lew Grade, Val Parnell, Norman Collins and Jamie Drummond, all of whom had executive or quasi-executive roles, were frequently at each other's throats, and tried to acquire information to further their personal aims. After a while I think Jack realised that I was smart enough not to divulge confidential information or drop him in the shit, and he began to use me discreetly to find out what some of the directors or senior staff were thinking.

When I arrived, Val Parnell was the managing director and Lew Grade was his deputy. But during 1962 Lew convinced the board to reverse their roles and eventually dispose of Val, who had been responsible for the Stoll/Moss theatre group when it was acquired by ATV. My first meeting with these two formidable figures was in the large office they shared, with their desks at either end. You entered through the door in the middle and turned left for Lew or right for Val, and you could say nothing to one without it being heard by the other. It was pretty scary, and a funny way to run a big business.

I saw more of Norman Collins and Jamie Drummond because Jamie, nominally the finance director, didn't have a clue about accounting, having spent most of his working life in a merchant bank which was a major supporter of ATV. That's how he landed the job. But he was a nice man who told me about his trips to New York, frequenting the jazz clubs in Harlem. He had no qualms about being a white guy in a black neighbourhood because he was a very big ex-rugby player unlikely to be intimidated by anyone.

Norman just loved to talk, and anybody within earshot would do. He was an author and, as an executive at the BBC, had risen to become the controller of television services. He left the BBC in 1950 and devoted his considerable energy to pushing legislation for the introduction of commercial television. When he discovered that I had read his post-war, best-selling novel, *London Belongs To Me*, he was delighted, and I was always made welcome in his office and given a coffee by his very upper-class secretary.

My boss Jack Gill shared space with the company secretary, Jack Barham. They had separate offices but their secretaries were in an ante-room outside, protected from the hoi-polloi (actually the accounts department) by a partition seven feet high. One had to brave interrogation from these two highly protective women before being invited into the inner sanctum.

The "two Jacks" were in their early forties, both qualified accountants, but that's where the similarities ended. Jack Gill was quiet and circumspect with his colleagues. As he came from Liverpool I think he felt a little intimidated by their exuberant personalities and backgrounds. Jack Barham, by contrast, was outgoing and said exactly what was on his mind. Once, after a long board meeting and lunch where the wine flowed liberally, the Jacks returned to their offices and Gill fell out of his chair asleep, into his very large wastepaper basket. Meanwhile Barham was not happy about something or other and causing havoc. I was called down, but arrived too late to stop him climbing over the partition – his secretary having locked the door to stop him from embarrassing himself in front of the staff – and setting off for Lew's office. We heard him shouting in the vein that the managing director was completely fucked. But Lew just calmed him down and took him back to his office, where he fell asleep too.

Most days went by without fireworks like that and I settled into a routine, getting to know the people in Accounts, one of whom was to have several major impacts on my career: Richard Robinson. Richard caught polio while doing his National Service in Trieste in 1954, which left him paralysed from the waist down. But that didn't stop this man of immense courage from winning a degree at Oxford, qualifying as a chartered accountant, getting married and having three children. Our relationship was fruitful and greatly reinforced when ATV bought Pye Records two years later.

John Monkhouse, brother of the better-known and since deceased Bob, who was a major face on television, appearing on panel shows and other entertainment programs, was the chief accountant, and although he appeared to be suspicious of me on my arrival he realised that I didn't have any oversight of his department and thus became more relaxed. I was soon enjoying a daily lunch in the staff canteen with him, Richard and other members of Jack Gill's team.

While I was at ATV there were several other acquisitions, including Gerry Anderson's AP Films. Gerry was already famous for his use of "supermarionation", most famously in *Thunderbirds*, the science fiction series that is still popular today. The supermarionation technique involved making reasonably life-like marionettes which could lip-synch to an off-screen voice, an invention way before Disney and others employed similar production concepts. Since their accounting function wasn't too robust – and their budgeting worse – I spent quite a bit of time at the AP Films studio which was great fun as Gerry, his wife Sylvia and the whole team welcomed me and let me watch several shoots.

Occasionally I also had to go to the Elstree Film Studios, of which my best (make that only) memory is of the *Emergency Ward 10* set and meeting the stars, Charles "Bud" Tingwell and Jill Thorpe, who played the senior surgeon and his very pretty nurse. The program ran for ten years with two thirty-minute episodes per week. Basically it was written, rehearsed and filmed on a full-time basis, frequently only a few days before being broadcast. Tingwell and Thorpe were amazing. They could be carrying on a conversation about the weather or what they were doing that evening, but when the director shouted *"Action!"* they immediately slipped into their roles. Bud of course was an Aussie and I met him again by chance – we were going to the same office block and he asked me for directions – about forty years later in Sydney.

Which brings us to what was, for me, the key acquisition made by ATV: Pye Records.

2. Pye: Welcome to the Record Industry

I SPENT forty-three years associated with music and worked in the UK, France and Australia. After starting out by accident in 1964, perhaps the dawn of a golden age for the industry itself and especially for London, I retired in 2007 at a time when it seemed to be facing momentous questions with few answers.

It's a career that included lengthy spells with four very different record companies, a time in publishing, and the embrace of Australia's oldest and biggest copyright protection society, where we looked after the rights of songwriters and their publishers. Along the way I wined and dined with celebrities and saw some of the biggest deal-makers in the history of the music business come and go.

It was an amazing rollercoaster ride that lasted four decades. But mostly this is a personal story of the people I worked with and the ones I encountered: some famous, and many forgotten. And it all began with the ten thousand pound company . . .

A noise – two people shouting – erupted outside my office at ATV.

At ten-thirty on a Monday morning, and on my floor, this was unusual as I was almost always the sole occupant. I was doing *The Daily Telegraph* crossword over a cup of coffee and the only person I had seen was Gladys, the tea-trolley lady.

I walked out and saw two men facing each other. One was medium height, balding, with a profile that irresistibly said "Fagin". The other was short, plump, with a round face in which the eyes disappeared in laughter lines. Welcome to Monty Presky and Alan Albert Freeman.

"May I ask what is going on?" I said in my best (Public School) voice.

"Who the fuck wants to know?" snapped back the taller one, Monty. "We're working out who's having which office and you're in the fucking way for a start."

Alan's face crinkled even further.

"We're your new neighbours," he said with a sly grin. "Pye Records. We're moving in next month."

An hour later I was asking Jack Gill for a relocation. A day later I got it. I didn't feel that Pye Records management were quite my kind of people.

* * *

Later I learned from Jack that ATV had bought fifty per cent of Pye Records for £10,000 with an option to buy the rest in ten years' time. ATV had also injected £400,000 into Pye, an astonishing amount for a small company, and it soon became apparent why.

Pye Records was a subsidiary of Pye of Cambridge, a brown and white goods conglomerate that, in the 1960s, spanned the world and had also brought in numerous technical innovations in sound engineering and broadcasting. Pye was the brainchild of a nuggety little Irishman, Charles Orr Stanley (although it was actually founded by William Pye in 1896), who had built an empire by manufacturing crystal radio sets in the 1920s. By 1964, things had got well out of control and Pye – and "C.O." as he liked to be called – was fighting for survival. Like many empire builders before and since, C.O. had failed to grow with his business or train a new generation to keep his company fit for the challenges ahead.

Pye Records and its best known label, Pye Nixa, had scored some very successful releases in jazz and pop: the early Petula Clark hit *Sailor* was produced by Alan Albert (known by this double first name to distinguish him from Alan "Fluff" Freeman, the TV and radio deejay). Pye was in those days looked at as *the* independent UK record company. As such, it was a major destination for overseas labels who could not get a licensing deal with one of the big three, EMI, Decca or Philips, or would rather not because their releases would be subordinated to those of the host company. Therefore Pye represented a number of American and European labels, including Frank Sinatra's Warner/Reprise and French Vogue, which had gems from Django Reinhardt and the Hot Club de Paris in its catalogue. Pye was also pioneering two major innovations: a low-price LP, "The Golden Guinea" series, at twenty-one shillings; and a unique delivery service through a fleet of vans direct to record shops.

Sales were high, margins were good, so what was the problem? Well the (very early model) computer hadn't worked for six months, few invoices had been sent out, some retailers were making payments on account, and many weren't paying at all. Pye Records had run out of cash.

It was obvious to Jack Gill that the £400,000 cash injection was a temporary reprieve. People with accounting and computer skills were needed for a massive and decisive catch-up operation. Richard Robinson, ATV's management accountant, was duly appointed Pye's finance director and asked that I join him as chief accountant. Both jobs were supposed to be temporary, with a promise of a rescue by ATV if things went terminally pear-shaped.

My temporary job lasted five years.

Welcome to the record industry!

3. 'Mr Benjamin Will Do'

MY first morning in the Pye Records accounts department was broken by a phone call.

"What's the balance?" said an unknown voice.

"What balance?" I enquired. "And if I may ask, who's speaking?"

"Louis Benjamin. Call me back," he said, and hung up.

That was my first contact with one of the half-dozen most famous people in the UK record industry in the '60s and '70s.

To his family and closest friends he was Louis; to his colleagues and business friends he was Benjie . . . and he chose which. Once, many years later at MIDEM, the annual international music industry conference at Cannes (which was not a real conference at all, but a knees-up for conversation, drinking and sex), one of our artist's managers asked me to arrange a meeting with him.

"Shall I call you Louis or Benjie?" asked the manager.

"Mr Benjamin will do," was the reply.

Over a decade and a half I got to know Benjie pretty well. We travelled together, we drank together and we played an awful lot of backgammon. He was loveable and frustrating, warm and penny-pinching, and sometimes almost brutally quick-witted, usually at the expense of Monty Presky or some other colleague. He may not have been the best boss I ever had but he was certainly the most fun. And fun was what a young guy rising through the music industry could find plenty of in the '60s.

Louis Benjamin came from a very modest Jewish background and saw show business as his quickest route to a better, more affluent life. In his teens he joined Moss Empires, the huge theatre group, and by the mid-'50s he was manager of the Morecambe Winter Gardens where variety acts and music hall vied for top billing. One story can sum up his management style – one of *his* stories.

When "All-In Wrestling Night" was introduced for Thursdays at the Winter Gardens, the bars were only allowed to open during the interval and after the last bout, until ten-thirty – two tight windows to cash in on the drinkers. One night Benjie came out of his office at ten, expecting to see punters heading from the auditorium to the bars. Instead he heard the MC announcing the main five-round bout was about to begin and rushed over to ringside.

"It's ten o'clock," he complained to the MC. "What the fuck are you doing to my bar takings?"

"Sorry, Mr Benjamin, I'll take care of it," said the MC, who was also the referee. He called the wrestlers together in the ring.

"The best of three falls or submissions or a knockout," he shouted. "Fight!" At which the Blue Corner came out and flattened the Red Corner with a monster king-hit.

"Knockout!" cried the ref – and the lads were in the bars by five past ten for twenty-five precious minutes of Benjie's bar takings.

*   *   *

Before joining Pye I hardly came across any Jews apart from Lew Grade, who became Sir Lew in 1969 and then Lord Grade in 1976. There was a Jewish boy at Eastbourne College – God knows why his parents sent him there, he was the only one – who didn't attend chapel, school or games on Saturday, and I don't remember ever speaking to him when I was there.

So I was totally unprepared to find so many Jews throughout the record business. Not only were several senior staff including Monty and Alan of the Jewish faith, it seemed so was every agent, manager and music publisher. At first I was daunted, but I quickly became captivated by their quick-fire repartee and single-minded pursuit of "the deal". Benjie, all of them, were obsessed by the need to make a deal – always on the best terms for them.

Take the Palladium deal. ATV controlled Stoll Theatres and Moss Empires, which included the Palladium that Benjie managed in addition to his duties at Pye. *Sunday Night at the London Palladium* with Bruce Forsyth was one of the highest rating shows on TV, giving entertainers enormous exposure. Managers would kill to get their artists on it . . . and that gave Pye a tasty carrot to dangle. It happened with several artists, Val Doonican, for instance. Benjie put him on *Sunday Night at the London Palladium* and in return, Val's manager signed him to Pye on terms that were very favourable for the label. Strictly speaking, it may not have been fair trading but everyone considered themselves a winner – and that was the essence of a good deal.

By the time Richard Robinson left Pye Records in early 1966 for the newly formed CBS UK company and I was promoted to finance director, I was used to being called into Benjie's office to calculate percentages, gross margins and net profits on the deals he was making daily. Fortunately I was good at mental arithmetic (this was in the days before pocket calculators) and formulas, and I got better as Benjie pitted me against Monty, who was fast and intuitive but often inaccurate. Benjie made no secret of delighting in seeing another Jew discomfited by a rather junior gentile.

It took Richard, me and a temporary staff of about thirty a year to untangle the accounting mess at Pye and put in some management routines. Only then did Benjie stop phoning me each morning for "the balance" – the balance of our bank account.

While working at Pye's base in Mitcham, I learned several salutary lessons, one of which was particularly important: my first experience of fraud. The accounting staff included a senior clerk who dealt with incoming invoices. Stan seemed like a nice reliable chap. He told us he had spent five years in a POW camp in Germany and now had a wife and a child, and we often went to a pub for lunch. One afternoon a supplier of maintenance materials rang and asked if he could see me after normal hours. When he arrived he told me the story and broke down. He had been sending Stan invoices for work that was never done and they were splitting the proceeds. I was devastated. Next morning I told my old boss Jack Gill. His advice was to suspend Stan immediately, tell him that a thorough audit was underway, and if there was any evidence of fraud the police would be informed. He also said Stan had probably been up to similar tricks before, and he was right. Stan was found guilty and lucky to avoid a prison sentence.

For me it was an experience which resonated nearly twenty years later.

Ten Per Cent Market Share

The Searchers' *Needles and Pins* went to Number 1 on the singles chart in my second week at Pye Records. They had already topped the charts in June 1963 with *Sweets for My Sweet* and gone to number two a few months later with *Sugar and Spice*. They were trading the top spot with the Beatles and we thought we were onto the real winners.

The Searchers, like John, Paul, George and Ringo, were four boys from Liverpool who looked good and sang pop songs everyone could sing along to . . . like "needles and pinsaa". Unfortunately most of their songs were cover versions. *Needles and Pins* was written by Sonny Bono of Sonny and Cher fame and first recorded by Jackie de Shannon, and after one more hit, *Don't Throw Your Love Away*, The Searchers slid inexorably down the charts, although they stayed popular in the northern clubs for several years.

Pye Records had a golden year in 1964: five number one singles from The Searchers (two), The Honeycombs, The Kinks, and the first from Sandie Shaw. Our five comprised 22 per cent of the industry total of twenty-three chart-toppers that year, an extraordinary achievement for a small label. In addition, Pye had several other top ten entries, including *Downtown* by Pet Clark, which was kept out of the top spot by Sandie Shaw and then The Supremes.

Pye was punching way above its weight in singles, which were such a significant part of the industry. EMI had 45 per cent of the total record market – made up of 45s, EPs and LPs – Decca had 35, and Pye and Philips had 10 ten per cent each. Suddenly we were the flavour of the month with ATV. By the end of the year we were making record profits and had cash in the bank.

It was a tradition to have a drinks party the evening a number one hit was gained or maintained, so there were at least twelve such parties at ATV House in Great Cumberland Place during

1964. Lew Grade would drop by, but never drink, to congratulate us, and often the tradition extended to number twos or number threes. As one of the youngest on the team I often mixed the drinks and got quite a reputation for my Bloody Marys.

Benjie's office was always the gathering place for work, celebrations, everything. Early every morning the senior managers dropped in for coffee made by the ever-present, ever-faithful and totally discreet Brenda Carr, Benjie's secretary. Brenda would have enough material for a few of her own volumes. She knew where all the bodies were buried.

Blond and blue-eyed but already running towards corpulence, the general manager, Les Cocks, was a charmer, particularly of women. Even my straitlaced Mother went girlish when he brought his adopted daughter to one of my son Jerry's birthday parties. "Hello, darling," he said, putting his arm round her and kissing her. "I've heard so much about you." Mother had also heard plenty about him but was still transfixed.

Les did his early training in selling himself at Hoover, where he was the top salesman for several years. "Always leave the ladies with a smile on their faces" had been his motto. He could have added, "and with a Hoover too, if possible". I didn't know his first wife but his second was Joan Turner, a comedienne and singer who worked in radio and TV and did the club circuit. She was a star turn. In the mid-sixties Les had a relationship with a gorgeous young woman at Pye called Pat and eventually married her after several huge, public bawlings-out by Joan. Present on one occasion, I was amazed at Joan's aim: she could have pitched for the New York Mets.

The other usual suspects who gathered in Benjie's office were Monty and Alan, Tom Grantham the sales director, and Peter Prince, the A&R man. While most of us had jobs with rather loose definitions, Les and Monty were there for ideas . . . and a reliable amount of abuse.

One morning in 1967, while reading the paper, Benjie said: "I see Geoff Bridge (then general manager at EMI Records) is out. He could be a useful man for us."

"What would that cunt do here?" asked Les.

"Your job," said Benjie, casually turning the page, and so it was.

Geoff Bridge did join Pye as GM and Les was temporarily on the outer. We never said Benjie's management skills included good succession planning. But Les did have some good ideas. Over coffee one morning he read about the postman delivering letters to Prince Charles at Trinity College, Cambridge, whose singing had earned some praise from the Prince. By the afternoon the postman was tracked down, brought into Pye's recording studio, and in less than a week a single by "The Singing Postman" was available at all good record stores. Not a huge hit, but a great story for the tabloids.

Later, the patriotic "I'm Backing Britain" campaign to boost the economy gave Les another idea. Bruce Forsyth was known and loved nationally through his weekly appearances on *Sunday Night at the London Palladium*, and his signature opening line. He would walk on stage, throw open his arms to the audience in welcome, and say: "Nice to see you." Then he would pause before bringing in the audience to say, "To see you . . . NICE!" It was mimicked by young and old alike. Tony Hatch wrote the *I'm Backing Britain* song and Tom Grantham and I went to the Wimbledon Empire where Bruce was appearing in a pantomime. In that evening's intermission he recorded the song on Pye's outside broadcast unit and within a couple of days the single was on the market.

Under Les's management one of the best features of Pye was its ability to distribute product fast. With its own studios, pressing plant and national delivery fleet it could have records in the shops within forty-eight hours of recording. For a while this was a regular feature of Pye's Top 10 Club. Devised and produced by Bill Wellings, a cover-version EP (extended play) of songs at the top of the charts was produced fortnightly. Recorded on Friday night, it would be in the shops by the following Tuesday.

Les left Pye Records in 1968 and later became a household name himself as the producer of ATV's *New Faces*, which was the first talent show on British TV where the winners were chosen by a panel of judges rather than by the audience. Amongst more famous "names", Tony Hatch achieved celebrity by playing the role of the harsh critic. On one occasion an unhappy viewer jumped into a cab taking Tony to Great Cumberland Place and threatened him with violence if he wasn't kinder to a particular songstress. Such is the power of television! *New Faces* became an immensely popular forerunner for later shows like *Britain's Got Talent*, and through it Les discovered Lenny Henry, the stand-up comedian who is now Sir Lenny, and many other future stars. As Bruce Forsyth would have said, "Didn't he do well?"

4. The Music Industry in the 1960s

THE sixties not only changed the world's taste for music, it was the decade that saw a whole class of industry insiders surging to new heights of power and prominence on the back of immensely creative singers and songwriters, and I crossed paths with plenty.

A(rtist) & R(epertoire) Managers

The A&R managers of the 1960s were the creative cutting edge of the record companies. It was their mission to discover and develop new talent, for which they were paid a salary. George Martin became the best known, probably in the world.

If they were lucky they also received a small percentage from the sales of their artist's records. As the decade went on the A&R managers began to realise that on their abilities lay the success of the record companies, so they started employing smart lawyers to negotiate deals giving them significant royalties and even freelance status, which enabled them to continue producing a successful artist if he or she changed labels.

Tony Hatch had joined Pye as an A&R man after doing National Service in the famous Guards regiment. His salary was less than some of the managers and his producer's percentage derisory. Furthermore, he was obliged to produce recordings of any artist as directed, such as "The Singing Postman", not a great career option. Tony was also signed to Welbeck Music (of which more later) as a songwriter on what would now be considered an unenforceable music publishing contract but which then was standard. Many other contemporary songwriters and producers later spent years getting themselves out of these one-sided contracts.

Tony was also used by Benjie as what can only be described as the "house accompanist". At a memorable dinner for Pye's overseas licensees, artist managers and VIPs – who amazingly included a beautifully preserved if unanimated Marlene Dietrich – Tony was asked to accompany the American comedian Alan Sherman as the after-dinner entertainment. No rehearsal had taken place. Tony and Alan had not even met beforehand, although Tony would have been familiar with some of Alan's repertoire, which consisted of clever lyrics to music adapted from well-known classical tunes. He had a huge hit in 1963 with *Hello Muddah! Hello Faddah!*, set to Ponchielli's *Dance of the Hours*. They were very funny songs and Pye sold a heap of his LPs.

Mr Sherman, however, thought he was a prima donna and acted like one. During the performance poor Tony was frequently berated by him for his perceived inability to follow the maestro's lead. It was not one of Tony's happier evenings.

A&R managers and directors were only "as good as their last hit", as the saying goes, and changed as frequently as the décor in the managing director's office. But some endured: George Martin, spectacularly, Norrie Paramor at EMI, and Cyril Stapleton at Decca and later Pye. Those two were from the old school, also band leaders who principally found new songs to record with their own vocalists, popularising them through nightly live performances and radio coverage, as well as by the sale of sheet music. The new breed of singer/songwriters, born in the late 1940s and 1950s, were just beginning to emerge.

The Singer/Songwriter

Until the 1960s, most recording artists were selected for their voices and looks and ability to perform songs supplied by professional writers to fit their stage personas.

Most record companies were slow to recognise the emerging superstars of the music industry. The rejection of the Beatles by A&R men and labels alike, most notably Decca who turned them down after they auditioned on New Year's Day, 1962, is an industry legend. The Fab Four were the most famous rejects but not the only ones.

Most managers looked first to sign their charges to EMI or Decca, who dominated the UK charts and had sales arms worldwide. It meant that any act approaching Pye for a record deal had probably been turned down elsewhere. But this changed with the growing perception, fuelled by Pye's chart success, that the two leaders were ponderous and set in their old-fashioned ways. They were still primarily interested in manufacturing white goods and brown goods, products such as radios, stereos and TV sets, a very large part of the electrical goods market, not catching the great wave of "youth power" that was about to crash over the record industry.

The Kinks have been described by social historian Dominic Sandford as "one of the most influential bands of the 1960s". I'd agree with that. But to many of us at Pye Records they were a pain in the neck – albeit a very profitable one. Between August 1964 and October 1967, they had twelve Top 10 hits including three Number 1s: *You Really Got Me* (August 1964), *Tired Of Waiting For You* (January 1965) and *Sunny Afternoon* (June 1966). But they are arguably best remembered for *Dedicated Follower Of Fashion* which became the theme song for "Swinging London" in 1966, and the sublime *Waterloo Sunset*.

I can't mention The Kinks without saying a bit about Ray Davies, a genius songwriter who went on to marry Chrissy Hynde of The Pretenders. He was the co-founder of the band with his brother Dave, and both the architect of their success and their demise. Ray's musical brilliance was undermined by his ungovernable temper. His outbursts of violence nearly landed him in court, and The Kinks were banned from the USA after their first visit.

So a pain in the neck? Absolutely – hey, they were big rock 'n' roll stars and expected to be treated as such. And they did make a lot of money for their record company and contribute to our salaries. But it was nothing for them or their managers to arrive at my office and demand an advance on royalties, or want to know how their latest single was selling in Canada.

The Kinks' managers were two of the new breed, aggressive types who went daily if necessary to their record companies to badger you for the impossible – and they almost always went away with something. Managers in general had twigged that, once their artists even looked like being successful, they were in the driving seat. Nothing could hurt an A&R man or a managing director more than to read a newspaper report that his top artist was defecting to another label, even if he was signed to you for another couple of years or two more albums. Then the MD's phone would start ringing: reporters, radio, even worse, his chairman, particularly if he was running the UK subsidiary of a US record company. The boot was moving uncomfortably onto the other foot.

One singer/songwriter I especially liked was Donovan. The press hailed him as "Britain's Bob Dylan", and with wistful and folksy singles like *Catch The Wind*, *Sunshine Superman* and *Mellow Yellow* he looked set for a long career. Dylan remains a world name today, still releasing songs. Donovan had a few more hits then slipped away after the '60s. Some might think he folded under the weight of the impossible Dylan comparison, but I think he just wanted to find peace. He was the son of a Scottish bus driver and he brought his dad to a reception for *Sunshine Superman*, which reached the number two chart spot on Pye. They were touchingly proud of each other, nice, down-to-earth people, and this quality probably helped Donovan cope with success . . . and give it away quietly, in his own time.

The Promotion Man

Every record company employed a "Head of Promotion" and in the 1960s Pye's was Johnny Wise, backed up by a young Issy Price.

Middle-aged, Jewish and not really knowledgeable about contemporary pop music, it was Johnny's job to get our new releases played on radio and television. In fact there was little pop music played on British radio in the early '60s because the BBC was the sole domestic broadcaster until the "pirates" – mostly ships anchored out in the North Sea – started what the government claimed were illegal commercial broadcasts. (Pirate radio was the setting for *The Boat That Rocked*, the 2009 comedy movie starring among others one of my favourites, Bill Nighy.)

Before the pirates, the station that anybody under forty listened to was Radio Luxembourg, run by the genial Englishman Geoffrey Everett. Though broadcasting from the principality of Luxembourg, the station had an office in London to handle the commercials it carried for British companies. The promotion teams from each record company fought for airplay because millions of young Englishmen and women listened to Radio Luxembourg's *Top 20 Parade* late on a Saturday night, which had a huge influence on sales.

Johnny was a lovely bloke who wore a "rug". One windy day it blew off his head and bowled down the street until our colleague Terry Stanley jumped on it. Johnny smacked it back on his head and no one said a word. Terry was a colourful East Ender, an accountant whose passion was gambling: horses, dogs, poker, roulette, you name it, he played it. A really great guy.

TV was also becoming increasingly important, particularly *Top of the Pops* which broadcast live performances each week to an audience of several million. Its success had a transformative impact on the BBC's adoption of "pop" programming as an important and relevant part of its charter.

"Promotion" was pretty clean in the UK in the early sixties but pressures were building up. The most famous promo man in the world was, and possibly still is, the American Alan Freed – the first record label guy ever to be convicted of bribing a DJ. He was definitely not the first to do it, just the first – and one of the few – to be "nicked" for the crime of "payola", paying a radio station to play a certain artist, which had long been an unsavoury practice in the music business.

After this infamous episode the promo man became more sophisticated. Goods, rather than cash, started changing hands and by the 1970s the "goods" were drugs. In Australia in the early '80s, the principal task of EMI's head of promotion seemed to be the acquisition and distribution of drugs to those to be influenced, more often than not at Benni's, a Kings Cross nightclub which was the hang-out of choice for the music and radio crowd.

Speaking of high times, I recall the day I was in the departure lounge at Sydney airport waiting for a domestic flight and a big name I knew came out of the cloakroom sniffing and pulling his nose with his right hand. He saw me and extended the same hand and we greeted each other briefly, before parting in opposite directions. My hand felt a bit gritty so I smelled it . . . and it wasn't soap. I washed immediately.

More refined ways of doing the business were developed in Europe. In Spain during the '70s, I was visiting several local record companies and noticed that on each CEO's office wall there were paintings which were clearly done by the same artist. Equally clearly, they were real crap.

"Who's the artist?" I asked.

"The painting is by Miguel X," was the reply. "He is the producer of the number one rock program on Spanish radio and he sells his paintings. They cost *mucho dinero*."

Radio has for many years been so formatted that most of the music played now is decided by a third-party programming company. It severely limits opportunities for the program producer or the DJ to include new releases, so the promo man and his record company have to find other ways of getting their material to listeners and buyers. It's all part of the modern world of the internet, YouTube and iTunes, which along with independent record labels has been causing the major record companies so much heartache.

But back to Johnny Wise and the 1960s.

Johnny was in hospital after his first heart attack and Benjie and Les visited him.

"Do you know how much airplay we've got since everyone knew I was in here?" said Johnny, proud of the sympathy his illness had generated.

"Yeah," quipped Benjie. "Just think how much we'd have got if you'd died."

Johnny did die a few years later. He and an era of decent, honest promo men passed away together.

Johnny was obviously not the guy the Rolling Stones were singing about in one of their early songs, *The Under Assistant West Coast Promotion Man* – a beach bum with an inflated ego who thought he was the key to a group's success.

Unfairly or not, I think they were echoing the thoughts of many bands in the sixties.

Music Publishers and Managers

In the 1960s, music publishers were almost looked upon as the enemy by record company executives: they took a fat royalty on all sales and seemed to do little for their money. Although the majors like EMI maintained their own music publishing arms, such as Keith Prowse Music, there was little contact or co-operation between them and publishers rarely assisted in the promotion of new releases. The record companies saw themselves as the natural leaders in the expanding music market, and this attitude did not change until well into the '70s.

Publishing is one of the oldest parts of the music business. Music was first hand-copied and then "published" in the 15th century when the printing press was invented. Queen Elizabeth the First granted licences to William Byrd and Thomas Tallis enabling them to reproduce copies of their compositions, presumably with a nice little kickback to Her Majesty. But the role of the music publisher only found its groove in the 19th century, when "popular" music, as distinct from liturgical (church) music, became available through sales of sheet music. An international agreement on the protection of rights for "authors" and a framework for the remuneration of their work was first embodied in a document which became known as the Berne Convention of 1886.

By the early 20th century the music publishers' principal job was to find singers and musicians to perform and record the creations of their own composers and songwriters. The concept of the singer/songwriter was decades distant, and popular songs of the day were allocated to individual singers or groups, chosen by record producers as much for their visual appeal as their vocal capabilities.

By the early 1960s Denmark Street, London's version of New York's Tin Pan Alley, was the flourishing hub of music publishing, and amongst the more prominent publishers was Cyril Simons, the managing director of MCA Music Publishing Limited, usually called MCA Music by industry people. MCA – which was a subsidiary of Universal, the American film studio – was used by several record companies to administer and exploit the publishing rights they acquired from their staff writers, both in the UK and overseas. While Pye Records did not use MCA, it did register Welbeck Music to administer the rights to songs by Tony Hatch and Jackie Trent and other writers and co-writers.

Cyril was a fiftyish bald guy with bulging blue eyes and a very semitic nose. He was overweight, overbearing, and better at stating a point than debating it. Rather surprisingly we all liked him because he would lapse into the self-deprecating humour which is a trademark of the New York Jewish comedians. He told us he was the ugliest kid in school and we believed him. Woody Allen could have modelled himself on Cyril.

But Cyril was a keen business brain who enjoyed a worldwide reputation and the ear of his American boss, Mike Maitland. For years MCA Music Publishing enjoyed a far greater share of business than the music rights in Universal's films generated.

After Herb Alpert and his business partner Jerry Moss formed A&M Records as the vehicle for a string of huge hits with dozens of acts, including the Tijuana Brass, the Sandpipers and the Carpenters – as well as Alpert's own classic love song, *This Guy's in Love with You* – their UK publishing interests were managed by Cyril through their company, Rondor Limited. This was a shelf company registered by two unknown people called Ronald and Dora. It wasn't until well into the seventies that Rondor became independent of MCA, under the management of Derek Green.

One of the many other publishers had gained fame by singing the theme song for the popular television series *The Adventures of Robin Hood*, starring Richard Greene. That vocalist extolling the exploits of the folk hero and his merry men was Dick James, who I came to know rather well – but that comes much later.

Tito Burns was the archetypal manager and booking agent and you could often find him in Louis Benjamin's office, not only because he was at one stage managing The Searchers. A professional accordionist, Tito was in jazz bands in his teens during the 1930s and continued playing after the war until he gave it away and took up full-time management and agency. One of his artists was the young Cliff Richard and later on he managed The Springfields (featuring Dusty) and Cat Stevens. His background in performance gave Tito a better understanding of his artists' professional needs, although this wasn't the case with The Searchers – they had a legendary break-up.

Tito, Cyril and Louis made a great trio of dealmakers, each highly competitive and dreading the possibility that one of the others would outsmart him. It was a lot of fun being the fly on the wall.

Eurovision

The Eurovision Song Contest started in 1956. The UK was not represented that year as its entry wasn't lodged in time, and a decade went by before the UK's first win.

In 1967, Pye Records artist Sandie Shaw won by a huge margin with *Puppet On A String*. So popular was the song with the Eurovision juries – only two countries failed to cast votes for it – and the UK public that it bulleted to No. 1 and stayed in the charts for eighteen weeks. Sandie was a nice straightforward Liverpool girl. With three chart-toppers (*Always Something There To Remind Me* and *Long Live Love* were the other two) and many other hits, she was a great contributor to Pye's bottom line over a five-year period.

Nine years later, in 1976, Pye "manufactured" another Eurovision winner with the Brotherhood of Man's *Save Your Kisses For Me*. In fairness, their manager Tony Hillyer created the Brotherhood: they looked good, they dressed well, their choreography was perfect and their song was simple. The lyrics repeated often enough for a peasant on the Lithuanian jury to understand. It worked, and gave Pye two of the five winners the United Kingdom has claimed in sixty-four years of Eurovision.

Both those wins came while I was at Pye, but the most exciting Eurovision experience for me was being at the 1974 competition held in Brighton.

The betting "book" which the musicians – probably the competitors too – held on the result had the Dutch entry, Mouth and McNeal, firm favourites with *I See a Star*. This duo had in my opinion, and as it turned out the juries' too, an average song, and their performance was uninspired. The group that stole the show and the prize and went on to become the biggest-sellers in the world was of course ABBA, with *Waterloo*.

Amazingly but shrewdly, ABBA's management had not signed a recording deal before their Eurovision appearance. As soon as they won a fierce bidding war broke out, won by the Epic label, part of CBS. The cost was high but the CBS general manager, Maurice (Obie) Oberstein, got the deal of a lifetime and nine number one singles in as many years.

The Eurovision Song Contest is now so big, with over forty countries participating in 2019, the glitz, staging and production so spectacular and the judging so obviously political, that nowadays winning songs frequently fail to even be released in many countries.

*　　*　　*

Most of the jobs at Pye were not as glamorous as those of the A&R and promotion teams. Mine certainly wasn't. As chief accountant I was based at the factory and distribution centre in Mitcham, a dismal little suburb in south London, where Richard and I shared an office (a bit like Lew Grade and Val Parnell but a lot less grand) and a secretary. In those days the company had more than three hundred employees, of whom only twenty-odd were at Great Cumberland Place. Forty were dotted about the country servicing sub-depots and their van salesmen in a few major cities.

Although our main task was to manually reconstruct all the outstanding sales invoices and help the computer team to implement new programs that would actually work, we also had to maintain all the other accounting records either by hand or on accounting machines. I had been to the headquarters of the major British computer manufacturers like ICT and Ferranti as a student and knew how computers worked in principle, but had no first-hand working knowledge.

So my promotion to Finance Director when Richard Robinson left in 1966 was a pleasing reward for the hard work I had put in at Mitcham over two years and another milestone in my career in the music industry. Now full-time in Great Cumberland Place, I began to meet and work with the people who would have a major influence on me for many years.

Benjie was the most important and I was frequently invited into his office, particularly if he wanted support in a meeting with a manager. This happened often when Petula Clark was there. If she was on her own, no problem – Benjie coped very well by himself. But if her husband/manager Claude Wolff came too, help would be needed. Actually, Pet tended to go into Benjie's office while Claude went to see Tony Hatch or someone else. Then Claude would join Pet, who would make an excuse and an exit, leaving Benjie alone with Claude. Brenda Carr would get a signal that help was required and send in a reinforcement. Pet was always delightful, and while I didn't mind Claude, he was a manager and they always wanted something MORE!

There were also frequent visits by artists and managers from the international labels represented by Pye Records. Sometimes we would hold a cocktail party for them in the beautiful rooftop apartment of Great Cumberland Place. To me the most memorable one was in early 1966 for the Reprise label whose president, Mo Ostin, brought along Nancy Sinatra, basking in the success of *These Boots Are Made For Walkin'*, as well as the songwriter, Lee Hazlewood. We kept the press away, so they were a happy and relaxed pair and I conversed with them as well as Mo, who was always a really nice guy and one of the first execs to be invited to our hotel when Benjie and I went to LA many years later.

5. Living in the Sixties

MOST of us who were around in the sixties didn't realise we were "swinging" until the media started telling us it was the Swinging Sixties towards the end of the decade.

However, we certainly had started to have a better time. After the austerity of the 1950s the British people were earning more, spending more and going out more. It was boom days for record companies as well as fashion boutiques and restaurants, and leisure pursuits like tenpin bowling. Currency restrictions were lifted, so more people were taking overseas holidays and many restrictive laws were amended or dumped.

One of the most important advances was the passage of the Sexual Offences Act 1967 which, after a decade of fierce debate, decriminalised homosexual acts between consenting adults or, more particularly, between consenting *male* adults. (The previous laws had either considered that lesbians didn't matter, or more probably that it was better not to mention them.) The new law cut off a very profitable source of revenue for blackmailers.

Another critical legislative change was the Theatres Act 1968, which removed the censorship of theatrical performances from the Lord Chamberlain's office. This overturned a law dating back to the early 18th century, giving draconian powers to a member of the monarch's staff to prevent performances that might "tend to deprave or corrupt" members of the audience. In practice this had become a prohibition of "bad language" and new ideas, and it also banned naked females from appearing on stage unless they stood stock still in "tableaux", which gave rise to the risible productions at the Windmill Theatre in London, whose motto during the war had been "We never closed", said with a lisp.

In 1958, Raymond's Revue Bar was opened as a private club to get around this law and became a very popular venue for people in the entertainment industry. Raymond's kept the nudity to striptease acts and had an evening for gays (Sundays), pretty tame stuff really compared with what was going on in many "erotic" clubs on the continent.

The club scene grew tremendously during the second half of the decade. There was the Playboy Club if you wanted your drinks served by girls dressed as bunnies; The Clermont if you wanted to gamble with the rich and famous; and my own favourite, Ronnie Scott's Jazz Club, if you wanted your jazz *cool*. That was where I first met Long John Baldry and heard him play twelve-string guitar. In 1968, Long John had an unexpected hit with *Let The Heartaches Begin* on Pye and I got to know him quite well: a talented and kind man who died young. And who was a totally unknown member of Long John's group, Bluesology? None other than a young Elton John, of whom more later.

*   *   *

In 1964, ATV was one of many large companies in London which had a staff canteen because there were few cheap restaurants around. By the end of the decade the canteen was closed and the West End had exploded with restaurants of all types and prices. I had my first Chinese meal in 1957 at the Hong Kong and Shanghai Restaurant in Shaftesbury Avenue. If I was trying to impress my girlfriend Liz, and I was, the outing was a complete failure as I had no idea what to order and had to leave it to the smirking waiter to decide for us.

However, it gave me my first taste of cuisine from the East and soon after that I tried my first Indian food at Veeraswamys, which has been looking down onto the southern end of Regent Street since 1926. This time I had consulted the menu in advance and confidently ordered my Madras curry, saffron rice, pappadums and so on. I don't remember who I was trying to impress but I'm pretty sure I did. By the time I was working in Great Cumberland

Place in 1966 the West End was full of every kind of restaurant and we frequented just about all of them.

Employers were starting to offer non-cash incentives including company cars as part of their senior staff packages and the era of the expense account lunch had dawned. The Mason's Arms in Seymour Street became a favourite haunt for many in the entertainment industry, and after work the Pye Records management would also congregate there. These were the days before random breath-testing, and one evening of heavy imbibing springs to mind.

The barman took a call and handed the phone to Tom Grantham.

"It's Harry," Tom said, hanging up. "He's totalled his car on the Albert Bridge and now he's in The Albert Arms."

"Let's go rescue him," we all decided.

We leaped into our cars and shot off across London on our mission. After a couple more drinks with an uninjured Harry (just to make *sure* he was alright, you understand) we decided to pick up our wives and take them *and* Harry out to dinner before dropping the poor bugger home. How we survived doing crazy things like that I will never know.

I guess the boutique owners were glad we did. Chelsea, in particular the Kings Road, was becoming the international centre of fashion and design, and even the most conservative of us took to wearing bell-bottom slacks. Ray Davies was singing about us. We were the dedicated followers of fashion.

*   *   *

Valerie and I were the proud parents of two kids and I vividly remember Juliet's seventh birthday party to which the whole of her class from Sutton Girls High School plus some extras were invited, about thirty in all. It was a beautiful day, we prepared games like "pass the parcel", and as they arrived the youngsters were sent into the garden while some of the parents had a cup of tea indoors. Suddenly we became aware of silence outside. Juliet was already practising two of her great skills, leadership and organisation. She was sitting cross-legged on the grass, with her guests neatly seated in a half-circle facing her, to hear her instructions for the next game.

Her young brother Jerry was similar, but with different skills. We had several short holidays with the Milan family at the Toorak Hotel in Torquay and Jerry was two when we bought him a sailor's suit. On wearing it into the dining room someone said, "What a smart boy!" Thereafter Jerry would walk into a room, seek out the most amply provided woman and approach her with a big smile and the words "me mart boy", before burying his head in her bosom. He was rarely rejected.

The children were becoming a lot of fun.

*   *   *

A few national and international events from the 1960s remain indelibly fresh in my memory.

For my generation the election of John F. Kennedy to the White House in 1960 was immensely important and encouraging. Here at last was a young, good-looking, articulate American at centre stage after more than a decade of Truman and Eisenhower. The Cuban missile crisis in 1962 was of huge concern. I remember being at Victoria Station and reading the *Evening Standard* which was seriously asking whether World War III was about to break out. That threat passed, but when Kennedy was assassinated in November 1963 the sadness and disappointment was profound. Valerie and I were arriving at a dinner party with some other married couples when the news came through, and no food was eaten. We all sat glued to the television and people cried. JFK's three years in the White House became known as "Camelot", and to us it seemed like a golden age. Perhaps now that we know more about the Kennedys the gap between our dreams and their realities is an even greater disappointment.

For once the British Government did not get sucked into an American war. From 1955 to 1975, successive US administrations maintained the "domino" theory that if one country in South-East Asia fell into communist hands the rest would follow, and spent billions of dollars fighting the Vietnam War at a cost of hundreds of thousands of lives. Perhaps it was America's treatment of Great Britain in 1956 over the Suez Crisis or just that we had enough on our plate, but public opinion was strongly against our involvement in Vietnam, with huge anti-war demos in London in 1968. Sadly the Australians backed the USA and many of their lives were lost or ruined too.

A sensational event in England totally captured the media and the nation in 1963: the Profumo Affair. It had all the best ingredients: sex, drugs, spies, chequebook journalism, the underworld, class and a suicide, which must have put a spike in the circulation of every newspaper. Fifty years later it still resonates – and should – because it exemplified so many of the insidious things about the "Establishment". In short, it involved a Cabinet minister (John Profumo) who was prepared to lie to Parliament about a sex scandal, specifically denying having an affair that had implications for national security, before being forced to resign; a vengeful "Christian" Home Secretary who felt himself to be the nation's moral guardian (Henry Brooke); the prosecution of a man for living off immoral earnings (Stephen Ward, who took his own life); a Lord Chief Justice (Hubert Lister Parker) who connived to have him convicted; bent cops who did their masters' bidding; and of course the two women at the heart of the scandal, Christine Keeler and Mandy Rice Davies. The "old boys club" was kept more or less intact throughout the Profumo Affair by the superiority and self-righteousness of the public schoolboys and "Oxbridge" graduates who were still in charge of things. Thank goodness those days are long behind us. Or are they?

The sixties was a monumental decade of social change in which we either participated or were swept along, and I will just mention three other events that captured the media and public attention during those ten years.

In July 1969, Neil Armstrong stepped out of an American spaceship and walked on the moon.

In November of that year the government passed a bill for the abolition of capital punishment in the United Kingdom.

And perhaps most surprising of all, England won the Football World Cup in 1966. What a decade!

By 1968, I was thirty-one years old though still by far the youngest of the senior managers at Pye Records. Valerie and I had two lovely children but we lost Giles, who was born in 1967 and sadly died after only a month. I was being reasonably well paid and we enjoyed holidays in England and Europe as well as outings to the theatre, cinemas and clubs, plus an ever-increasing circle of party-loving friends. We were part of Swinging London! So why was I bored? I don't know the answer but I found a solution: PARIS!

6. Paris! With CBS

IN the late autumn of 1968, I received a phone call from Richard Robinson who was now at CBS Records in London: "CBS International are setting up a European office in Paris and looking for a finance director. Would you be interested?" I certainly was. Apart from London the two cities I wanted to work in were Paris and New York. This could be a promising start.

I was offered an interview with Peter de Rougemont, the head of CBS International in Europe, and we met at his office in rue Freycinet, a three-minute walk from the Seine. This must have once been a beautiful old 16th arrondissement family home, four floors plus a basement. Through an old carriage gate you entered a cobbled courtyard just big enough to park two cars. CBS Disques and the associated April Music occupied the ground and first two floors while "we" were on the top floor. The basement contained "the canteen", as they called it, which was a three-star gourmet dining room seating about thirty, plus the kitchen. Here I learned why lunch was so important to the French.

De Rougemont was in his late forties and he had spent most of his career in South America. Despite the name he was in fact very English, coming over as fussy and pedantic yet rather timid – that was him to a tee. He didn't want to waste time or money on a lengthy recruitment search, and within an hour or so I had been offered the job, which I accepted. Public School, working for Price Waterhouse, then spending five years as a chief accountant before becoming finance director in a record company – that did the trick. To de Rougemont, I was straight out of Central Casting.

Pay and conditions were acceptable, and it was agreed that until July I would be staying in the London office while spending the occasional week in Paris. Preliminary visits to CBS affiliates in Germany, Austria, Switzerland, Holland and Belgium would be arranged, but not to CBS Italia, which was an interesting exclusion in the light of events ten years later. My main focus was on helping the European offices set up the monthly financial reporting packages required by CBS in New York, review them, and get them into HQ on time. Simple!

The delayed transfer to Paris allowed Juliet and Jerry to finish the English school year and gave Valerie and me time to find French schools and somewhere to live. She was excited about Paris too.

Saying goodbye to everyone at Pye Records was not easy. I had made some terrific friends there, I was working in the most exciting city in the world and in one of the hottest companies in the music industry. But I knew this was the right career move at the right time.

*　　*　　*

Moving into a temporary small office at the CBS London premises in Theobalds Road was a bit of a comedown, but I was on the same floor as Ken Glancy, the American managing director, Maurice "Obie" Oberstein, the marketing and sales director, and Richard Robinson. I was soon back in Paris to meet the two other top CBS International executives, Nic Demey who co-ordinated marketing and Denis Puisseux who would work with me on getting compatible computer systems installed in each affiliate.

CBS had established branches in Europe by either taking back its American repertoire and establishing an independent subsidiary company, or buying the local licensees. This latter approach was often successful, but the buyouts could prove to be inordinately difficult to inculcate into the "CBS way". Invariably their senior management came as part of the package, entrenched in outdated habits and questionable ways of thinking. They did not take kindly to being told what to do or how, despite being paid a tidy sum for the goodwill of their business.

The worst was Holland. The Dutch at best are often inflexible, and Aart Naujoks lives in my memory as the most bloody-minded and unobliging finance man I have ever met, incompetent to boot.

Concreted in his ways, Aart refused to make any concessions, modify any systems or attempt to implement the CBS reporting requirements. Months of discussions and arguments followed until, to my disgust, de Rougemont called me into his office one day to tell me I was effectively banned from the Amsterdam office. He let Naujoks get away with it. My initial assessment of my boss was spot on.

But all the other companies and finance people were fine, and later in the year my American boss, Nick Cirillo, joined me for a tour of the European operations. Nick was a great second-generation American who still spoke Italian with his parents in the Bronx, always happy as long as he was regularly supplied with "cawfie and cookies".

Monsieur Ziegler was the finance director of CBS Disques and although – or perhaps because – he was old enough to be my father he treated me with haughty disdain (very 16th arrondissement) but let me get on and work with his staff. Indeed, he helped me get my work permit – and what a bloody saga that was.

A foreign employee in France had to have both a residence permit and a work permit. This was long before the UK joined the EU. Once the applications – huge dossiers, with every English document including my Father's and Mother's wedding certificate professionally translated into French – were lodged I had to check into my local *Préfecture* every month for a questioning in front of many other people about . . . just about anything. It could be a bit humiliating. The situation turned into a Gordian knot: no residence could be granted until I had proof of valid employment, and there could be no work permit without proof of legal residence.

Monsieur Ziegler knew someone high up in the Department of Employment and got me an appointment with an official who was charming, unhurried and quite friendly. When we started discussing the CBS catalogue he admitted his love for 18th century classical music and I saw my chance.

"Ah, Monsieur," I said in French. "Would it be possible for me to offer you some of our recordings? We have some fine ones."

He looked shocked.

"Mais non! It would be quite improper for me to accept."

I imagine that chagrin would have described the look on my face. I had just clumsily tried to bribe a senior public servant and probably buggered my chances of getting a work permit for good. I was lost for words.

He looked at this pathetic Englishman, smiled and said: "But of course, if these records were given to my daughter that would be another matter entirely."

Work and residence permits were forthcoming and the beautiful sound of Pierre Boulez conducting the New Philharmonia Orchestra in Debussy's *La Mer* could be heard floating through the open windows of another lovely Paris apartment.

Our recent experiences with the French bureaucracy lead me to believe that not much has changed in half a century. But that's a different story for another day . . .

*   *   *

Valerie came over to Paris and we started to look for schools and an apartment. Our intention had been to live in central Paris as close as possible to the chosen school. We felt that Juliet and Jerry needed to keep getting their lessons in English while they experienced life in France, so they couldn't go to just any school.

The choices narrowed down to an English school that catered exclusively for expats, the American school in the western suburbs, and the Lycée International at St Germain-en-Laye, which was quite a way out of Paris. It provided basic schooling in French, but gave students of each nationality at least ten hours of lessons a week in their native language. This was the one we chose. The Lycée had been set up after World War II for the children of officers and enlisted men under the aegis of SHAPE, Supreme Headquarters Allied Powers in Europe.

While looking for an apartment in the vicinity we discovered Parly2, a huge residential project destined eventually to house twenty-five thousand people near the north-east corner of

Versailles which had a shopping centre with restaurants, bars and cinemas. Parly2 was the biggest complex of its type in France, probably Europe, and on opening day it caused a traffic jam all the way back to Paris, over twenty kilometres. The apartment blocks, four and five storeys, were built in clusters, each with their own identity for features like garden design. The apartments were fitted out with modern appliances, and as well as car parking, a swimming pool and tennis courts, the blocks had their own *conçierges*. The freshness and sophistication of this suburban development illustrates how, by comparison, tired old Paris had fallen way behind the UK and USA in urban planning and domestic upgrading.

The property owners were the developers themselves, who had a vested interest in keeping the first influx of tenants happy while they continued building, and hence the rents were low at Parly2. It also had a school bus service to the Lycée, so we thought it was perfect. Despite M. Ziegler's disapproval – he felt that one could *only* live in the ninth arrondissement – we snapped up an apartment. When the school term finished in July 1969 and our house in Carshalton was sold we had one last large party for all our friends. It was the beautiful evening of the twentieth and everyone wanted to watch the television. Why? Just as we were about to land in France two intrepid Americans had landed on the moon.

*   *   *

Harvey Schein was a mover and shaker at CBS and I came to know him quite well. CBS was huge in the United States, owning one of the two biggest television and radio networks, but its record division was almost an afterthought until "music" took off as a major consumer product in the '60s.

Goddard ("Call me God", and everyone did) Lieberson was in charge at CBS Records and he had done very well for his employers by persuading them to put money into Broadway shows in return for the music reproduction rights. His two offsiders were Clive Davis who ran CBS Records USA and Harvey

Schein who ran the recently formed CBS International. CBS was the first of the major American record companies to think they could make more money by both exploiting their own catalogue overseas instead of taking royalties from licensees like EMI and Decca, and competing for the emerging talent in those foreign markets. They were right.

Harvey was a tough, Jewish New York lawyer. He had done a few years in the CBS legal department and negotiated several good deals before being picked by Lieberson to head up the new division. He was literate, numerate and a good listener. He was also extremely handsome and loved travelling, particularly if he had to meet attractive young women. He was perfect for the part.

One of the most interesting parts of my job was to follow up on potential acquisitions, as the plan was to have a CBS affiliate in every country in Western Europe by the early '70s. When I joined there were plenty of unfilled spaces on the map, so one country where I became very involved was Spain.

In 1970, General Franco was still ruling Spain. Being virulently anti-communist, he had been invited into NATO by the United States and the two countries had become quite close. There was certainly no barrier to US – or UK – firms doing business in Spain. The country was, however, a dictatorship and run as such: business standards were to say the least several rungs below those of the Anglo-Saxon world.

As usual, CBS International first looked to establish itself by buying out the Spanish licensee, a small, privately owned company in Barcelona. The outlines of a deal were drafted between Harvey, the CBS lawyers and the two owners, and I was sent in to look at the books, what would now be called "due diligence".

The owners were ordered to give me access to *all* the information I asked for, so at the outset I was told that two sets of books were kept: one for management and one for the tax inspectors and other "official" purposes. It was a nightmare trying to rationalise or authenticate anything. I'll give you two examples. Firstly, the rate at which they paid mechanical copyright royalties (i.e. what was due to the songwriters and music publishers from record sales) to the Spanish collecting society was based on sales declared in the "official" books, barely half of the amount due from the real sales. This was probably also true for the payment of artist royalties but more difficult to establish without going through every contract. Secondly, the profits declared for tax, which were assessed by the State of Catalonia on a regional basis for the record industry as a whole and then divided pro-rata to declared sales among the individual companies, showed that EMI was paying over *ninety* per cent of the tax total and the Spanish companies combined less than ten per cent. The more I looked, the more I found, and the more I began to worry, because I knew how much Harvey wanted to buy this company.

After ploughing through this mess for two weeks I decided that enough was enough. I also decided not to say anything to de Rougemont. Knowing what a wimp he was, he would have taken me off the case and filed a bland whitewash report.

Therefore I invited myself into the owners' office and told them the figures did not add up – and why. This was just before lunch which, being summer, was followed by a siesta, with the office closed until five-thirty p.m. The owners asked me to come back and see them that evening, and I had a rather restless afternoon in my hotel trying to read *I Claudius* by Robert Graves.

After the siesta I was asked by Senor A, the owner in charge of administration, to join him and his partner in a private office. I was shown through a door covered by a bookcase, down a flight of stairs into a basement that appeared to be full of personnel I had never seen before. Momentarily I was a little scared – this is a bit too near the city sewers, I thought!

Senor B greeted me, we sat down, and they tried to explain it all – by producing the *third* set of books! Quite how the system worked I never really discovered. Suffice to say I knew the deal was not going to happen. CBS, a Top 100 company in the States, could not allow a business it owned to be run like that, and, as I pointed out in my report, this one could not suddenly become "clean". Too many questions would be asked about the past and CBS could be liable for huge penalties.

41

Almost nobody was pleased. The owners lost a buyer and later the CBS repertoire. Harvey wasn't pleased because he was getting on famously with Senor A's daughter. De Rougemont wasn't pleased because Harvey wasn't. But perhaps the CBS tax and legal departments were pleased as it saved them from a huge headache. And I think Nick Cirillo was pleased because it saved him going to a country where he couldn't easily get "cawfie and cookies".

A few months later we opened Discos CBS in Madrid, hired a lovely South American guy as MD, put in *one* set of books, and hired Coopers to do regular audits and produce CBS-style management accounts. And everybody was pleased again.

*   *   *

We made some great friends during our two-year stay in Parly2. Most of the other residents were like us, both the locals and couples from different nationalities: either not expecting to stay very long, unable to afford to live in central Paris, or preferring effervescent Parly's cosmopolitan lifestyle.

Although living outside Paris meant a forty-minute commute by car for me each morning and evening, we were within walking distance of the Parc of the Palace of Versailles which we used extensively after our third child, Lucy, arrived in October 1970, and we had the best shopping facilities France could offer. The Lycée Internationale seemed to work well for Juliet. Not for Jerry though, and with great reluctance we booked him into boarding school back in the UK. And then the wheel of change turned for me again. Ken Glancy, the boss of CBS Records in London, announced that he wanted to go back to the USA.

To most of us who were intimate with the London operation there seemed only one internal replacement choice. Obie Oberstein had long been seen as Ken's number two and he was running an extremely successful marketing and sales division, as well as having a role in product supply and distribution. Although he was an American, he had made it clear that he had no intention of returning to the States. Out of the blue it was announced that

Richard Robinson had also put his name forward, and he and Obie would both be interviewed in Paris by a panel made up of Harvey, Jacques Souplet, the French managing director, de Rougemont and, for some reason, me. I think I was there on the pretext of helping Souplet who always – untruthfully – claimed not to speak or comprehend English if Harvey was present.

Some time in May 1971 the interviews took place. Richard was great: on time, full of ideas and very articulate. He had met and talked with Harvey many times of course. They got on well and spoke the same language. Obie was awful: late for the interview after having a very good lunch, he treated Harvey as if he knew nothing about the UK market and made us all feel uncomfortable. I also sensed a latent antagonism between them. Both were Jewish New Yorkers, but one trained at law school and the other originally as an engineer. And there seemed to be something about Obie's ongoing bachelorhood that did not sit well, although no aspersions were cast.

Richard got the job and Obie stayed on in his existing role.

Still in May, I had to go to London and Richard invited me to dinner. Never one for beating about the bush, he said he was doing some restructuring and intended to create the senior position of director of operations, covering product supply, distribution and a new function, building and running the recording studio planned for Whitgift Street. Obie would be concentrating on marketing and sales, so would I like the new job?

My feelings were mixed. I loved being in Paris, but after two and a half years the job was becoming repetitive and de Rougemont wasn't going to increase its scope. This new position was very hands-on and it would be another great experience. Valerie and the children were happy, we packed our bags again, said goodbye to our friends in Paris, and headed back to England.

Richard Robinson was having a very big effect on my life, and it didn't stop there.

7. Back to London

AFTER a memorable holiday in Ibiza we were back in London. Well not exactly London. Because of the speed of our return I had to find a furnished rental until we bought a flat or house and this was quite difficult. Furnished places for two adults with three children were either unbearably small or very expensive, and I had to settle on a house at Bray near Windsor, about twenty-five miles from London. This meant a long drive to work and back, with the added complication of getting Juliet to Wimbledon High School. We solved that by having her temporarily "boarded" four nights a week with a friend's family. Jerry started as a boarder at Ascham, the prep school for Eastbourne College.

We had decided to look for a flat to buy in Wimbledon, and after Valerie spent a lot of time searching we found Manor Fields in Putney, an early 20th century development of four-storey mansion blocks set on ten acres around beautiful gardens, with access to Putney Heath and Wimbledon Common. It was and probably still is absolutely lovely.

Meanwhile, I was working back at Theobalds Road, now as one of the senior team, learning all about a new job from scratch.

The CBS Records factory was at Aylesbury, forty miles out of London, the distribution depot was just north of the Euston Road, and we were building a recording studio in the West End, so my job was not going to get done sitting in head office. Fortunately the years travelling through Europe had relieved me of any residual shyness and I soon got around to meeting the staff at our three locations. I had to co-ordinate the production of records and cassettes and related printed materials, keep the factory at full production, and ensure the distribution depot received, processed and expedited incoming orders. In theory I knew it all.

Normally I had to be in HO for weekly production and marketing meetings, and management meetings whenever. It was also important to liaise with A&R director Mike Smith (who used to produce The Tremeloes) so I could keep track of upcoming releases, to chime in with Obie for marketing plans, and to see Richard just to stay in the picture.

My new colleagues welcomed me warmly. I think some of them had found Obie a bit difficult to cope with. He certainly tried a few tricks on me, but we had a very frank talk soon after my arrival and from then on we became solid business friends. Obie was always supportive – he just liked to see how far he could push everyone.

At the distribution depot Vic Ridgewell kept a soldierly eye on things. I'm sure he resented this young fellow coming in to boss him around, but when he saw that wasn't my style he relaxed. Vic led a very efficient operation.

*   *   *

Johnny Nash, Johnny Cash, Manitas de Plata, Tony Bennett and Andy Williams are just some of the names I'm going to drop now. Working for CBS in London in the early '70s was an open sesame to many of the greats in the business. But I'll start with this.

"Excuse me, Mr Witt." It was our uniformed retired serviceman who manned the front door and had just interrupted a promotions meeting. "But I've got a scruffy little bloke downstairs asking for you. Says 'is name is Simon."

It had to be Paul Simon. And he *was* dressed casually, even for a world star.

In the early '70s, American music was competing with and often losing out to British rock 'n' roll. American recording artists were not always greeted warmly by the UK record giants, EMI and Decca, to whom their home recording company had licensed them. Suddenly there was a CBS company waiting for them with open arms in London, shortly to be followed by RCA and Warners (initially known as Kinney, their controlling company). The difference was that the big two UK companies had so much local talent on their rosters that the label and product managers were overloaded. They coped badly with the foreigners, and with their own executive management. On top of that, Sir Joseph Lockwood and Sir John Read at EMI and Sir Edward Lewis at Decca were far too preoccupied with the other industries their conglomerates were into. (EMI stood for Electric and Musical Industries.) They also came from a stuffy generation disinterested in modern pop culture, which they neither understood nor liked.

So CBS UK under Ken Glancy, an American who talked their language, and then Richard, was a favoured destination for US-based recording artists like Paul Simon who were touring or visiting the UK. Moreover, it became a second possible home for emerging UK talent who felt their efforts might be overwhelmed on the major British labels.

In 1972, a young American reggae singer from Houston made a comeback single, *I Can See Clearly Now*. It was a big hit in the United States and although it only got to number five in the UK charts the song gave him a base for his number one hit in 1975, *Tears On My Pillow*. Johnny Nash came to London to promote *I Can See Clearly Now*. He looked lonely and spent a lot of time in the CBS offices, so we all got to know him and I'd take him out to lunch. I never thought to quiz him about Houston, but at the time I had no inkling that one day I would be marrying someone from that city. I remember Johnny very clearly: he was nice and friendly but homesick.

Johnny Cash was a different kettle of fish. He toured the UK and Europe in 1972 and I saw him at Festival Hall in London. Afterwards we gave him and the Carter Family a dinner in the Hall's restaurant. The Man in Black was in great form both on stage – "Good evening, my name is Johnny Cash," followed by *Folsom Prison Blues* – and off. But for once Derek Witt our promotions manager, who was in charge on evenings like this, had failed to make a simple enquiry: "What will you have to drink?" We all knew that Johnny, June and the family were teetotallers, but when he asked for "milk, please" it was a surprise – and a problem. The kitchen had no fresh milk, it was after eleven o'clock, and milk was difficult to find at that hour, even in London.

A junior promo man was sent out in search and came back with a bottle after tapping a mate of his who was the night porter at a hotel.

The dinner was a delight. I was sitting next to June Carter who talked quite a bit about life on the road for the "family" while Johnny mostly listened to her. After performing a major concert and staying until midnight they were the perfect guests.

Not all visiting celebrities were so happy and amiable. Tony Bennett recorded *I Left My Heart In San Francisco* in 1962 and had since gone without another major hit. By 1971 he was living in London – he left CBS in 1972 – and both his career and his morale were at a low ebb. Derek and I took him to The Cheshire Cheese in Little Essex Street for lunch one day and, for once, we were told not to spend too much. CBS didn't want to open the purse strings for him. Years before I had loved and danced to his recordings, and it was sad to see how depressed he had become. But it is uplifting to know that he fought his way back to stay in good spirits well into his nineties.

Becoming involved with the artists was mostly a pleasure and a reward, though secondary to getting the job done, and that wasn't always easy. A couple of things come to mind regarding our distribution depot. Firstly, the early 1970s saw the build-up of the IRA terror campaign and everyone became conscious of security. CBS distribution kept on receiving phone warnings that a bomb had been planted in the depot, which once caused us to shut down entirely until the Bomb Squad had been right through it. The fact that it was almost certainly a disgruntled neighbour – or maybe another record company – did not help.

The other incident was nearly disastrous. Our IT department was small but vital to the shipping and invoicing of product sold to nearly three thousand retailers in the UK. Peter, the son of a high-ranking union official, was the manager, a talented software developer, but highly strung and a bad communicator. One day he locked himself in the computer room and threatened to wreck it. He was having a complete breakdown, so it was a relief when Vic Ridgewell talked him out. Our systems were in great danger as

Peter had no proper back-up in place. Another lesson learned, or maybe two.

*   *   *

One of the company highlights was our annual conference. In 1972, Richard decided to hold it in Ireland at a hotel on the outskirts of Killarney. We flew to Dublin and transferred to a private train – perhaps the Irish were too smart to let sixty-odd record company executives loose on a regular service. It was dusk when we disembarked to be told the hotel was a fifteen-minute walk away. This came after learning on the train that there was a national power strike in the republic. We wondered how that would affect our stay, and I think we were mainly worried about the supply of ice for our drinks.

Out of the fading light three figures emerged.

"Who is being the boss around here?" asked the biggest one. We all pointed at Richard in his wheelchair. "And you're welcome to Killarney, sor. But I have to tell you we've done a deal with the local power men. They'll switch on the juice tonight for your dinner and tomorrow at seven a.m. But it'll be off again by twelve until around six. And tomorrow we're goin' to switch on the power in the Killarney dance hall at around ten in the evenin'. We've been told you'll be havin' a wee party there. And now I'll be wishin' you a foin stay."

And they melted away.

The conference went very well in the circumstances. We went horse-riding the next afternoon but the highlight was the evening in Killarney. The Zombies had had a big hit with *She's Not There* in 1965 and two members of the band, Paul Atkinson and Hugh Grundy, now worked for CBS. When the lights came on in the dance hall they joined some other band members on stage and about ten thousand youngsters from Killarney saw the lights, heard the music and came pouring in. It was one of the greatest spontaneous shows I've ever been to.

*   *   *

Harvey Schein left CBS Records International in 1972 to head up the CBS/Sony affiliate and in 1973 Clive Davis was kicked out of his position as president of CBS Records. Clive had been instrumental in turning CBS from a classical and stage albums recording company into a major rock label. His ego was enormous. I attended a conference of CBS staff and executives at Grosvenor House in London, and for three nights running Clive took to the stage and was applauded and cheered for minutes on end. One of my English colleagues whispered, "Bit like a Nuremburg rally, isn't it?" But I guess you could forgive the ego because his reputation for picking and promoting new artists was legendary. It was probably his ego that got him fired, although it was alleged that he paid for his son's *bar mitzvah* with company funds.

So for reasons that seemed totally obscure then – and still do – a member of the CBS law division was promoted to replace Davis. Walter Yetnikoff has written an "apologia", *Howling at the Moon*, in which he tries to explain why he was such an arsehole, but he doesn't really do himself justice: he was much worse than he makes out. The few times I met him he was off his head on cocaine and surrounded by a coterie of devotees.

That year Peter de Rougemont brought us the bad news that Walter was sidelining Richard to an administrative position and bringing in Dick Asher, another member of the law department, as CEO of CBS Records UK.

Dick duly arrived with his Jewish Princess, two children and a personal secretary, and immediately demanded a Rolls-Royce with chauffeur. This was fair enough because Richard had a chauffeur, but on arrival the JP immediately complained about the saloon's lack of space and the RR-trained chauffeur. His duties were not too onerous – driving Dick to work and the kids to school and most days taking the JP shopping – but there were certain protocols which chauffeurs had to follow and one was at Harrods. Chauffeurs had to drop their passengers off in Brompton Road, drive round the back to park, and wait to be recalled by a link-man. After a few weeks this was not good enough for the JP – and

I have the following verbatim from the chauffeur and, slightly embellished, from my boss's wife.

He: "I'll be dropping you off here then, ma'am, just get the doorman to call me when you're ready."

She: "Today I'm just going in and out really fast. Just park and wait for me here."

He: "You know I can't do that, Mrs Asher. I'll just be round the corner."

She: "I'm telling you to wait for me here – and that's an order."

The chauffeur comes round to open the kerbside door and hands her the car keys.

He: "Sorry, Mrs Asher, but I'm a professional chauffeur. If you want to park here you should have the keys."

Then there's a phone call from the JP to Dick and he calls me in. I managed to keep a straight face in his office, but the cheer that went up when I told those outside what was happening might have been heard at Harrods. The next chauffeur we hired was David, who was not RR-trained but seemed, shall we say, to fulfil a number of Mrs Asher's special requirements.

Dick didn't interfere much on operational matters, which was good for me, concerning himself with new talent deals and looking after incoming CBS execs and artists. He apparently liked to dictate (this was in the days of shorthand and typewriters) long reports to Yetnikoff after lunch, and often his hard-working secretary would emerge from his office looking quite exhausted and even dishevelled.

During this time the new studio complex at Whitgift Street was completed and Andy Williams became the first singer to use it. He was a true gentleman whose manager only asked that a glass of champagne be ready for him before he started the session. Andy also did an Albert Hall concert and afterwards attended a dinner for about three hundred people. Following the main course he insisted that our head of promotion took him to every table and introduced him to every single guest whom *he* thanked for being there. A great memory of a great artist.

*   *   *

Another very different artist was Manitas de Plata who only recorded one album for CBS, in 1972, but did an Albert Hall concert with his brothers that year. He was brilliant: playing *flamenco*, he captured his audience with his handling of the guitar. Born in the south of France at Sete in a gypsy family, he was self-taught and an absolute devotee of Django Reinhardt.

For some reason it fell to me to take him and his extensive entourage out to dinner one evening, so Valerie and I chose a small restaurant in Kensington, persuading the management to let us have it exclusively for the night. Manitas liked its intimacy and spoke extensively in French to Valerie and me about his early life. He also displayed another talent – he was an extremely good caricature artist. But his eldest brother was a nightmare who spent most of the evening leaving his table to cater to the desires of some ardent young female fans who had gathered outside. Maybe he was only signing autographs . . .

* * *

During my five years with CBS I covered practically every aspect of the record business except signing and recording new artists, so I wanted to have a go at negotiating. I had seen the master (Louis Benjamin) doing deals and reckoned I could handle it. But Dick Asher turned me down flat, saying "You have to be a lawyer." Such an obvious bit of crap wasn't exactly motivating, but my next brush with him was worse.

The studio was having problems with a well-known American recording manager. He would only come in to record late at night, he was perpetually stoned, and he insisted on using coke openly. Very little was getting done. One by one our engineers refused to work with him and at last threatened to close the studio down. I took the problem to Dick, pointed out the facts, and said that if the police raided the joint everyone there could be found guilty of criminal conduct. His response: "Aw, get real. This is the music business." I was out scouting for a new job the same day.

As a footnote, I heard that the American manager died soon afterwards. Fortunately the studio staff had managed to get him into a taxi first.

8. Pye Records . . . Again

I HAD never lost touch with Louis Benjamin or some of my other old chums at Pye, so I knew he wanted to cut down on his travel and workload to concentrate on his main love: running the Stoll/Moss theatre group.

The record company was in good shape: it had several incoming licences from the United States and Europe and the Pye catalogue, in turn, was represented by licensees in the major territories around the world. So I rang Benjie, told him I had left CBS and was looking for a new gig, and he called me over for lunch. We nutted out a job description and I was offered the position of sales and international director, responsible for the UK sales team and all international relationships. It sounded like a dream job and in many respects it was. I asked Tom Grantham, the previous sales director, for his opinion and he was for it – at sixty, he was looking to retire early – as was his number two, Roy O'Dwyer. The only fly in the ointment might be Walter Woyda, who had been brought in as general manager after running the cassette manufacturing plant, but what Benjie wanted Benjie almost always got and Walter agreed, or probably just gave in. I got the job, starting ASAP. It was a real pleasure saying goodbye to Dick Asher and I didn't bother too much about *mes adieux* to the Jewish Princess.

Rejoining Pye Records after five years was a bit like marrying the same girl again: you could immediately remember why you were in love, but fairly soon you remembered why you had broken up. Most of the old gang had left: Les Cocks to run *New Faces*, Ian Ralfini and Terry Stanley to set up Warner/Reprise, Monty Presky and Alan Albert Freeman to pursue other ventures. I inherited Harry Castle, export manager, Peter Gooch, international manager, and the sales team. But it was a great challenge and I would be working closely and travelling with Benjie.

Pye still enjoyed a good reputation and a significant artist roster, although it had become a bit middle-of-the road with Max Bygraves, Des O'Connor and Val Doonican, all of whom appeared regularly at the Palladium or another theatre in the Stoll/Moss group. These artists sold hundreds of thousands of LPs, the most successful being the *Singalongamax* series. First released in 1972, it continued for several years.

In 1973, Benjie and I went to the press opening for the MGM Grand in Las Vegas. It was my first trip to the United States and I was off to the launch of the biggest hotel in the world. We flew to Los Angeles in a Pan Am Boeing 747, and to say I was impressed by the upper deck lounge/dining room where first-class passengers could ask to have their seats would be an understatement. Over the next few years I met some fascinating people in that elite "bubble". Everyone talked to everyone else and I spoke with Texas oilmen, all sorts of businessmen, even a young Central African politician, who was later assassinated. Benjie loved it. When he was tired of talking we'd play backgammon.

The Beverly Hills Hotel was the meeting place of choice for the music industry, in the daytime at a cabana around the pool where food and drinks were served and in the evenings at the Polo Lounge where, in those days, the *maitre d'* was a dwarf with an incredible memory for faces and names. He always had a table for Mr Benjamin and his guests.

During our stay we met many of the industry's top people, such as Mike Maitland from MCA and Mo Ostin and Joe Smith from Warner/Reprise, two companies with whom Pye had licensing deals. I did score one coup. On leaving the hotel one morning I spotted Goddard Lieberson from CBS waiting for a car and introduced him to Benjie. Even he was impressed to be meeting God.

We went on to Las Vegas and stayed at the Sands Hotel which used to be the mecca for The Rat Pack, but by '73 it had fallen from favour although some great acts still played there. We were looked after by a man Benjie had met many years earlier, an ex-SAS officer with the British forces in Korea who got involved with *The Little Angels of Korea* touring show, which was how he landed in Vegas, where he had evidently become the police force tutor in unarmed combat. I wouldn't have wanted to take him on or his chauffeur-cum-bodyguard, a young South Korean with a body that looked as tough as steel and flexible as a whip. He drove us wherever Benjie wanted and took us to the head of every queue for a show, where he'd whisper something into the doorman's ear that would always get us shown to a "house" table.

At the opening of the MGM Grand I met Kirk Kerkorian, the president of the hotel chain, and saw a show that had Debbie Reynolds as the *commère* and Siegfried and Roy as the headline act – probably the greatest illusionists of their era. Benjie met Debbie but I didn't.

On the Sunday, Benjie wanted to relax by the pool so I was chauffeured into the Nevada desert alone to see the Hoover Dam. I was getting used to being a celebrity, if only a minor one.

*　　　*　　　*

Benjie and I made several trips together, mostly to New York where we stayed at the Sherry Netherland on 5th Avenue right by Central Park. It was, and probably still is, one of the great hotels from the 1920s. Once there the routine was always the same: drop my bag in my room, then go down to Benjie's suite where a list of telephone numbers was waiting for me. My job was to call up everyone Benjie knew in New York and arrange meetings, lunches and drinks. He wasn't big on dinner, preferring to get a hamburger and go to a theatre.

On the list would be Morris Levy. He ran Roulette Records, to whom Pye occasionally licensed a UK artist. Morris was known to have affiliations with the Mafia – he was eventually convicted of extortion – and Benjie would say, "Just tell him I'm in town if he wants to see me." Morris was pleasant on the phone but always "busy just now".

On the sixteenth of April, 1975, we flew into JFK and as usual were picked up by Irving Chezar, Pye's "Man in New York". Irving appeared to do little except worry about the condition of his wife who had cancer and the cost of healthcare, but he had an amazing network of contacts in the worlds of entertainment and music. This time he couldn't wait to tell us about the previous night's opening of an off-Broadway musical, *A Chorus Line*. Benjie said we had to go that evening to the second performance and Irving pulled out all the stops. We were met at the Public Theatre by the manager, who apologised for not having one seat left but said if we crept in as the lights went down we could sit on the stairs. Thank heavens for the lack of health and safety regulations in those days.

What a show! After decades of Rodgers & Hammerstein musicals here was something completely different. I've seen *A Chorus Line* several times but I still remember that first one. Benjie was so impressed that he sourced the sheet music, flew it to London, and Pye had a cover version of the showstopper, *What I Did For Love*, recorded and released within a week. Regrettably it didn't chart. But hey, that's showbiz.

*   *   *

We also took several trips to France, mostly to catch up with Leon Cabat and his "family" at Vogue Records. Leon was a fascinating man and I wish I had been able to draw out more of his story. I do know that during the Nazi Occupation, Leon was involved with Charles Delaunay in running the Hot Club de France, a front for the Resistance movement. In 1947, they set up Vogue Records.

Vogue had recorded many now-famous names, including Django Reinhardt and Stephane Grappelli. It was at the forefront of "hot" jazz which had been popular in France and America for several years while England was tied to "trad" as played by Kenny Ball, Chris Barber and other jazz bands, most of whom had been around since the '50s, playing a version of the pre-war "Dixie" style.

Being in Paris on Pye Records business didn't deter Benjie from pursuing his other objective, finding new talent for his West End shows, so we were regular visitors to the Lido and similar nightspots. Benjie always knew the manager and we were usually invited backstage or, in the case of the Lido, upstairs, wending our way through the fans and feathers of the chorus girls. It was always business, business, business . . . but Benjie did enjoy mixing business with a little bit of pleasure.

MIDEM, the international music industry trade fair (Marche International du Disque et de L'Edition Musicale), started in Cannes in 1967 and was attended by thousands of (mostly) men from record and music publishing companies and independent labels, as well as artists, managers and producers. The big record outfits booked stands, like a motor show, where they would entertain and show off their recording artists. The first time I was there, 1974, Pye had a stand with a waterfall. We stayed at the Mediterranée, which was a bit quieter than the Carlton, the biggest and most popular hotel on La Croisette. One trick you learned very quickly was never to tell the waiters your room number. You just wrote it on the chit if you didn't want to wake up next morning and find that you had bought an awful lot of rounds for total strangers.

Some business did get done at MIDEM, and it was a great opportunity to catch up with your overseas affiliates as well as meeting new people in the industry.

One small anecdote may be enough to demonstrate Benjie's talent as a negotiator. Monty Luftner was the CEO of Ariola, the very successful Munich-based German record company. Benjie wanted a licensing deal, but Monty was full of himself and difficult to bring to an agreement. However, he played backgammon and Benjie challenged him to a match, I suspect the best of five, over lunch at the Mediterranée. The deciding game was progressing with no obvious advantage to either player when Benjie made a move that was right out of character. I may have sucked in my breath, as Benjie looked up at me and his eyes said, "Don't say a word." Minutes later Monty was so thrilled to have beaten an acknowledged expert that he put out his hand and the deal was done!

*   *   *

Working at Pye again was not all fun and trips, however. I had a sales budget as well as incoming licensing and distribution arrangements to manage, and one of the most interesting UK deals was with DJM Records, a label whose major and only star was a young Elton John. I seem to remember that he had an eight-album deal which was coming to an end. DJM sold huge quantities of all eight albums and the "Greatest Hits" compilations, but they were trying to find a replacement for Elton and therefore spending a lot of time and money recording other artists.

DJM was owned and run by none other than Dick James (who sang that *Robin Hood* theme song), a veteran music publisher, and he had recently brought his son Stephen in to head up the record division. Over a two-year period I saw a lot of them both and met Elton on a number of occasions. He was always very pleasant except when he had his Glaswegian manager and partner with him, the demanding and always disagreeable John Reid. Elton dumped him as a lover later on and then as his business manager when the books didn't balance.

Although a lot of the work and travel at Pye was enjoyable I was finding Walter Woyda less and less rewarding to work with, and he probably thought the same about me. Whereas Benjie was generally a "big picture" man, Walter was a micro-manager who had been successful running a cassette plant but had little idea about the long-term needs of a record label.

And so it was that I made the one big mistake in my career. I was persuaded to join Dick James Music as general manager of the record company.

The package was the killer. My salary practically doubled and I was given a Jaguar XJ12 as my company car plus a generous expense allowance. What girl could turn down an offer like that?

9. Off-key with Dick James

EVERYTHING started well: a nice office and seemingly a young and enthusiastic team, lots of hopeful talent coming into the studios, but so far no success in breaking a new artist.

DJM even had a foothold in the USA, with Arthur Braun and Carmen LaRosa looking after the publishing and the records respectively while Lenny Silver handled distribution. Lenny also had a retail company in Buffalo, New York, but getting the records into shops was not the problem – all product was on one hundred per cent sale or return in the USA in those days. The hard part was getting airplay.

DJM signed an American singer/songwriter who had a small following but was virtually unknown outside the States: Johnny "Guitar" Watson (the self-announced "Gangsta of Love"). His first album on the DJM label, *Ain't That A Bitch*, was released in 1976 and eventually (it took years) sold over half a million copies in the USA, a great achievement.

I went to the United States on several occasions with Stephen James, which usually entailed visits to New York, Buffalo and Los Angeles. One time we supported Johnny at his concerts and partied afterwards. In Buffalo, the party finished up in my room, not by invitation, and I guessed that the band had decided they were less likely to be raided there than in their own rooms. By the time they were all smoking joints or snorting cocaine and two couples were copulating on the floor I decided that this was more than enough and I wasn't going to be the apparent host if we were busted. I quietly left the room and went out to find a taxi. Surprisingly, it wasn't all that hard for a man with no luggage to find a room even at three a.m. in Buffalo.

By contrast, I loved Chicago. We went there to see Papa John Creach, a jazz and blues violinist who played with Jefferson

Airplane, Jefferson Starship and other bands. He didn't make it as a solo artist but he was a great performer and I was sorry to only see him once.

Back in London, Stephen was trying hard to break a new artist but he kept getting distracted by "big names" in other fields, as well as involving himself – and inevitably me – in various sideline activities, which is how I came to discover that we were sponsors of Formula Ford racing, and recording such celebrities as the British heavyweight champion, Henry Cooper. You will doubtless remember that huge flop, *'Enery The Eighth I Am I Am*. Henry was a really nice bloke who should have stayed in the boxing ring.

We also recorded Dennis Waterman, who was well known for his co-starring role in *The Sweeney*. His records didn't make it until he took *I Could Be So Good For You* to EMI and scored quite a hit in 1980. From the few times I met him Dennis seemed a pretty nice guy too.

Although my job description did not require me to be responsible for the financial management of DJM Records, my background and the fact that I was general manager ensured that I would demand an overview of how the company was doing. I became concerned with a number of issues that were never discussed. First, the practice of charging expenses to the accounts of signed artists without their written acknowledgement. This meant there were growing unrecovered and unrecoverable costs showing on the balance sheet as "Artists' Advances", on top of which the operational costs were being under-disclosed.

Even more worrying was the deal set up in the United States whereby royalties earned were passed through two related companies before the percentage payable to the artist/songwriter was calculated. I had no knowledge of the negotiations with Elton John when his contracts were set up, but it seemed unlikely that he or his management were aware of this at the time. Elton eventually took Dick James to court in the 1980s and received back royalties of more than seven million pounds.

My love affair with DJM was going sour, and when Dick took me to task for some of Stephen's deals and activities it was time to go.

I severed my ties with Dick James and early 1978 saw me in my first period of unemployment.

10. Interlude

WHEN I left DJM I had a wife and three children. Juliet was nearly seventeen and about to take her "A" Levels, Jerry was coming up to fifteen and reasonably happy at Eastbourne College, and Lucy was seven, in a prep school before going on to Putney High. We owned a nice flat in Manor Fields and had just bought a cottage in the quaint village of Nunney in Somerset. We owed some money certainly, but not too much to worry about. I was confident of getting another job and Valerie had rejoined the workforce with a firm of architects in London.

I decided that I needed some time out and went down to the cottage for a few days, immersing myself in renovations and convivial evenings in the pub where I got to know the locals, including our neighbour across the road, Alan.

Nunney, a hamlet for centuries, had one of the most photographed thatched-roof cottages in the west of England, sitting on the corner of the main street where a bridge crossed over a stream. This was usually placid, but occasionally it flooded the houses built on the lower banks and a small castle which, for some obscure reason, had been built at the bottom of a hill. Its wall facing the hill still lies in ruins, and therein also lies a rather odd slice of local history. During the Civil War the castle was occupied by Royalists until a contingent of Roundheads turned up and began firing their cannon down the hill. The Royalist commander surrendered his castle and his troops as the wall came down, but for some other obscure reason the victors allowed him to go free provided he stayed in the village, which he did. He built himself a charming cottage on the riverbank opposite the castle and lived on.

It was easy to while away the time at Nunney but I had to give some thought to earning money again.

I had made many friends in the music business and several were willing to help me out, including one who lent me a desk, a room and a telephone in an office in the West End. I was soon offering my services to anyone who could use me and pay me, and some people did. As a precautionary measure I also signed on as an accountant to a specialist employment agency and was overwhelmed by short-term job offers.

The one where I had most fun was the Japanese bank which had set up a joint venture with a London trading bank to deal in forward exchange rates. They kept good records of all their transactions – what they wanted was someone to tell them how much money they had made. Having spent five years turning incomplete records into meaningful sets of accounts, this was no great task for me. What made it unusual was the young Japanese traders asking me what the profit result would be. I decided that we could have a bit of fun and suggested they make forecasts, which were put up on the trading board.

The evening before my much anticipated announcement their second most senior trader came to see me.

"Do you have forecast from Mr Hirohito?" he asked. "He is boss, very experienced, should win. No win, lose face."

And, I thought, I might lose more than face. Very quietly next morning I slipped Mr H. the result – or close to it – and there it was, up on the board. Everyone was thrilled that Mr H. won and he and his senior team took me out to a lunch where I must admit I got to like sake. An enjoyable and well-paid interlude.

I could have happily continued doing consultancy and temporary jobs, and that summer they gave us the opportunity of spending some very pleasant times at the cottage. Then the phone rang and another phase of my work-life opened up. This was the call that took me back to Europe and eventually to Australia with a second wife, but none of that was foreseen at the time. It was in a future quite far away . . .

11. E(very) M(istake) I(maginable)

BY 1978, EMI was known in the music business as Every Mistake Imaginable and had done much to deserve it.

While it was unarguably the biggest and most successful record company in the world, with one of the most famous trademarks of the 20th century – Nipper the dog looking at a gramophone horn – and gold-plated labels including Columbia and Parlophone, EMI had its weak points. And one of the weakest was Capitol Records, the wholly owned American subsidiary which in theory was answerable to EMI Limited in London.

However, Capitol was run by Bhaskar Menon – an Indian educated at Oxford who could talk for hours but was unable to take a decision, as well as being averse to confrontation – and a bunch of insular Californians who saw little opportunity outside their home state, and certainly nothing outside the USA. This caused them to concentrate on a narrow if sometimes successful roster of American middle-of-the-road artists, and they were unimpressed when their British counterparts came up with great rock 'n' roll talent. (Would you believe they refused to release the first Beatles singles?) Capitol finally got behind some UK acts and huge profits did ensue . . . for a while.

Sir Joseph Lockwood, who had done a great job in the 1960s, stepped down as CEO in 1970 and EMI replaced him with Sir John Read, who had run the Trustee Savings Bank. He was a money man – and there was plenty in the kitty. So Sir John decided to "diversify". That meant he bought anything in the wider consumer market that was up for sale: the Blackpool Tower, pubs, clubs and hotels to name but a few. This might not ultimately have mattered, but he also tried to take the "scanner" into America.

The CAT-scan was a genuine EMI invention: it took X-rays of the brain and was a worldwide first. Many British businessmen would have sought American partners to open up the huge potential of the US medical market, but Sir John chose to take on the giants like General Electric by setting up EMI Stateside and marketing the scanners direct. It was doomed from the start. Lobbied by the American electronics giants, President Jimmy Carter introduced legislation limiting the importation of medical equipment. General Electric ignored the patent, developed its own scanner and got away with it, only having to pay paltry damages a decade later.

In the 1970s EMI was forced to sell off all the Read acquisitions, often at heavy losses, and by 1978 the company was close to bankruptcy.

*   *   *

EMI Music was the organisation formed in 1978 to oversee more than thirty music companies worldwide. Although headquartered in Gloucester Place in London, it was decided to promote Bhaskar Menon to head up the new operation from his office in Los Angeles. This was typical of EMI Group management. Sir John Read, now the chairman, knew nothing and cared little about the music industry, which was by far the most important division in the group.

That phone call I just mentioned came from Clive May, inviting me to lunch at a pub in Mayfair. I saw Clive often, usually at dinner with our wives and other friends, so this was unusual. At the time he was finance director of EMI Limited (the parent company quoted on the stock exchange) and had good relationships with the top EMI people, including L.G. Wood (a previous MD) and John Read.

Clive put his thoughts in a nutshell: EMI Music needed a finance director for Europe and I needed a job. I was soon being interviewed by Tony Todman, the finance director for EMI Music, and Leslie Hill, managing director for Europe. By mid-1978, I was sitting in a nice basement office in Gloucester Place with the task of reviewing the financial management and accounting functions

65

of fourteen companies spread across Europe, from Finland to Italy and from Spain to Greece. Thank you, Clive.

In essence, my task was similar to my responsibilities at CBS but the nature and culture of the EMI companies were very different. Most had been set up before the Second World War. Several had been through a succession of English executives in charge. And there was an overall lack of "worldwide cohesion": they did pretty much whatever they liked. Now EMI Music was here to start putting its unifying objectives and requirements into action.

With London designated as the world headquarters for EMI Music, staff were hired, seconded and transferred to fill the necessary positions to overview its management: the legal, financial, computing and operational aspects of all companies in the music group. But as usual with the decisions of EMI's chiefs there were some exceptions. Gloucester Place did not oversee artist acquisition and development. That was left largely to the individual companies, with interference from Capitol in Los Angeles and EMI Records in London, a separate entity. Nor did we have much say in the running of those two companies, the most important in the whole music group. As so often happens, the concept of a good business structure was marred by its less than universal implementation: another classic EMI mistake.

Still, I wasn't about to complain. I had a very agreeable boss of my own age and we had complementary skills – he was a much better financial manager, but knew nothing about the music business. His first goal was to get the balance sheets of all the companies into better shape by releasing unproductive assets, reducing debt and generally improving the ratio of net assets. My task was to help the individual finance managers achieve this.

*   *   *

I had been at Gloucester Place a few months when the phone rang one day and the caller told me I was wanted over at Manchester Square, the longtime headquarters of EMI.

"By whom?" I asked.

"I don't know, but they asked for the most senior person in the finance team and Tony's on holiday. They're waiting for you in Room 203."

On arrival I recognised the chief accountant from EMI Limited. The other three men were strangers.

"We're from Gulf and Western," one announced, "and this meeting is totally confidential. Can you give me your word that none of what we discuss will be divulged to any other person? Your future job may well depend on this."

"Well," I said, "it rather depends on what we talk about."

This guy not only looked like a thug but sounded like one.

The upshot was that Sir Bernard Delfont, a board member of EMI Limited and brother of Lew Grade, had been in discussions with Paramount, a subsidiary of G&W, with a view to them taking a fifty per cent interest in EMI and this team were with us to start the due diligence.

After the meeting I contacted Tony Todman and Leslie Hill to find out what information I could divulge, and I kept my job.

Nothing came of the Paramount interest but then Thorn Limited came into play, just in time. It was common knowledge inside EMI that the company was forecast to run out of funds within weeks, so the acquisition and merger of the two companies into Thorn EMI Limited came as a relief – at least in the short term.

*   *   *

The day-to-day operations at Gloucester Place were routine, but overall my colleagues were helpful and pleasant. I had a delightful and efficient assistant, Jochen Frese, based in Cologne, who had spent a few years in Switzerland when the "Central European" EMI HQ was based in Zug, yet another bizarre decision. Jochen knew all the finance managers – and where some of the bodies were buried – spoke excellent English, and was generally well liked and respected. In looks he was the perfect Aryan with blond hair and blue eyes, but there the comparison ended. He was softly spoken and almost gentle. I think we hit it off immediately.

I also had a delightful PA. Pauline was from the Caribbean, and she had been a professional backing singer. She'd toured with Stevie Wonder amongst others and told hilarious stories about how he would run his hands over his female group so that he could "see" them better. She was now married and lived in a "black" part of Fulham with her husband and small son. As I lived in Putney I occasionally gave her a lift home, and one day she asked if we could pick up her son from school. We stopped and saw this flood of children aged seven and eight coming out.

"De problem wiv dese black kids is dey all look de same," she said, cracking me up.

The fourteen EMI companies under my umbrella as finance director for Europe were grouped into three divisions. Central Division comprised Germany, Austria, Switzerland, Holland and Belgium, overseen by Wilf Jung in Cologne. Southern Division included France, Spain, Italy, Greece and later Portugal, overseen by François Minchin in Paris. The Scandinavia Division was made up of Sweden, Norway, Denmark and Finland, overseen by Anders Holmsted in Stockholm. I was to see lots of these three gentlemen and their operations over the next five years and came to like all of them due, possibly, to their very different personalities.

Wilf Jung was a pre-war German child who had hung around the occupying US Forces in Frankfurt. He was street-smart, charming and spoke excellent American.

François Minchin was another sort of charmer. Considerably older, he had been in Pathé Marconi (the EMI subsidiary) before the war and knew all the greats from that era, including Edith Piaf. He was very affable but more attuned to the old EMI business model of putting "nice chaps" in charge of companies rather than the best suited.

Anders was a big Swede with a major eating disorder who loved parties and drinking and ice hockey. But he was a good operator and kept his four companies on their toes.

For the next five years I spent a lot of time travelling around Europe, with the occasional trip to New York or Los Angeles for a conference thrown in. Whilst the work could be a bit repetitive there was always a drama happening somewhere. For instance, a major fire in the record factory in Cologne, which led to the decision that LP production for Europe would be concentrated on Uden in the south of Holland. That was where I first met Jean Panther, who gets a lot of billing later on.

One particular event stands out and rather sadly exemplifies the character of EMI and its management in those days. I received a call from Magnoli, the finance director of EMI Italia. He told me unbidden that his MD had instructed him to make some payments for personal expenses – school fees – which were not authorised under his contract. This MD, John B., was an Englishman who had spent his working life with EMI in increasingly senior roles and been promoted from Italy to the position of managing director of EMI Records, the UK company, only weeks before.

Why Magnoli told me this I still have no idea, but it caused a storm. Having alerted François Minchin, Jochen and I flew to the Italian company near Milan. Our preliminary talks with Magnoli alerted us to other discrepancies, and after an initial audit we took back to London and Cologne as much of the financial records and other paperwork as we could carry. Remember, this was 1981 and not everything was computerised.

Over the next three weeks Jochen and I found more and more to question. Not just the unauthorised payments of the MD's personal expenses but other areas of doubt: such as why, uniquely, EMI Italia never appeared to sell off its deletions (overstocks), and the factory was using about thirty per cent more raw materials and fuel for LP production than the other EMI factories. It boiled down to one answer: the management at EMI Italia were all involved in company-wide scams.

After another visit to Milan, this time with François, Magnoli broke down and spilled enough beans for us to fire virtually all the senior management on the spot. They didn't argue. It was leave now and don't look for compensation or we'll bring in the police. They were all implicated in fraud, theft, or the cover-up, and this certainly included John B.

When I got back to Gloucester Place, Bhaskar was there and I requested an immediate one-to-one meeting. I gave him the key facts and the evidence we had against John B. At this, Bhaskar threw up his hands.

"Oh no, not again!" he said.

"What do you mean by 'again'?" I asked.

"Oh, he did the same thing when he was MD in Mexico."

I remembered two things at that moment: Jack Gill's tip about the habits of repeat fraudsters, and some advice from a management consultant, who said "Never lose your temper – but sometimes it pays to simulate anger."

I knew I would never beat Bhaskar in an argument, so it was hit him first and hard.

"So", I said, "you have knowingly promoted a criminal twice and you didn't even think of warning your fucking finance director? I demand that you fire John B. and have him out of his office this afternoon. If you don't I shall seek a personal interview with the chairman of EMI immediately."

That worked.

It was an interesting yet saddening experience that has probably unfairly left me with a jaundiced view of Italian work ethics.

In 1982, the government in Portugal was radically changed and the country became an interesting place for foreign investment, so once again I set off to discuss the possibility of buying out EMI's local licensee and turning his business into a fully owned subsidiary. Lisbon is a beautiful city – its hills and trams reminded me of San Francisco – and the licensee was the head of the delightful Carvalhao family, who greeted me with great courtesy and frequently entertained me in their boardroom for lunch and took me out to dinner. Their company ran every aspect of the music business except manufacturing and included a charming, old-fashioned record shop in the heart of the city. The buyout looked promising until problems similar to those I had uncovered in Spain ten years earlier appeared, so the purchase did not go through.

Speaking of Spain, as mentioned earlier EMI was based in Barcelona with its own factory and distribution centre and a strong catalogue of local artists. But it was run by an indecisive young Frenchman who had been put in place by François Minchin because he was "the son of one of my friends". Perhaps not quite the most important qualification for an organisation employing several hundred people in an era of sustained industrial unrest. On one occasion I was being driven into the factory and, looking up at the top floor, I saw a large banner with MUERTE AL INGLES written on it, *DEATH TO THE ENGLISHMAN*.

"Which Englishman are they upset with?" I asked.

"Well you're the only one here and they think you're planning redundancies," came the reply. And that was what we were planning, but everyone stayed calm and I left before the workers' threat was put into effect.

Despite hiccups like that, Jean and I still love Barcelona and the Catalans. A few years ago it was where we last saw Jorg, Jean's delightful brother-in-law. He was wheelchair-bound but still witty and full of energy. Sadly he died soon afterwards.

*   *   *

A few more stories about the "management" (if you can call it that) of EMI Music.

One: Visits to London by Bhaskar were, as far as we could tell, timed to allow him to talk at us until the early hours of the morning. Once, after a dinner that started at around ten p.m., some of the European MDs and I and our wives were invited back to the flat he had rented in Bond Street. Bhaskar asked the ladies to excuse their husbands for a final discussion. When we emerged it was nearly three a.m and the girls, including Mrs Menon, were asleep in the sitting room.

Two: By 1980, Leslie Hill had quit and Ken East was number two to Bhaskar, fully in charge of worldwide operations at Gloucester Place. We got on okay and he frequently invited me into his office to give me his thoughts on the European companies, but I knew he had a terrible temper. One evening after Ken and I had been going through the budgets of the Central European companies with Wilf Jung and the MDs we were all invited to Ken's flat in Pimlico for drinks and finger food. The flat was in a semi-basement in a beautiful Victorian house and we were greeted by Mrs Dolly East. Everything went well for the first hour or so, then Dolly took exception to someone's remark and flew off the handle, followed by Ken going off at her. Wilf and I decided that discretion was the better part of valour so we backed up the stairs and sat on the top step, ready to make a run for it.

Three: Ken called me over to his office. His nose was very red, a bad sign. He told me that the day before he and Dolly had been on Jack Gill's cruiser on the Thames where gin and tonics were liberally consumed. Ken left the boat and went back to his car; Dolly said she was going on to London with Jack. She didn't come home, but in the early hours Ken got a call from the local nick. He could hear Dolly screaming abuse and was told that she was under arrest for assaulting a police officer. Could he pick her up? He did so reluctantly and I could easily imagine their walk home.

*   *   *

In September 1982, Jean and I got together. We rented a flat in Pimlico and then moved to something a bit larger in North Kensington. EMI management were incredibly helpful, particularly Wilf Jung, Jean's boss in Cologne, who talked Peter Andre, the head of classical music, into putting Jean on his staff at Gloucester Place. She had all the qualifications and more for the job and it looked like we would be happily living and working together in London for the foreseeable future.

But then of course events – fate if you like – took another turn.

*   *   *

EMI Australia was one of the old Commonwealth subsidiaries invariably run by an expat Englishman, but the government had done a one-eighty-degree turnabout in the previous decade or so. Far from offering more ten-pound tickets to encourage Poms to emigrate, it now limited work visas to three years, and Peter Jamieson had six months to go at the helm. The search for his successor was on and my boss, Tony Todman, was the preferred candidate.

In January 1983, Tony flew to Sydney to look over the job and the management and get a feel for the place. As mentioned, Tony was a great bloke who would have got on famously with the sports-mad locals, but he wasn't really into the music business. Furthermore, he had just fallen in love with a friend of ours – our first landlady.

When he returned to London he told Bhaskar and Ken East that he couldn't take the appointment. As usual, the EMI top brass looked around, briefly, and said to themselves, "We were going to promote Nick Hampton to Tony's job in London, so why don't we give him the gig in Australia?" They must have mulled over that decision for at least . . . well, all of five minutes.

So (it all happened the same morning) I was called up to Bhaskar's office and promised the job on one condition: I had to be in Sydney by the twenty-third of March.

That evening I took Jean to a favourite restaurant. In my pocket I had a piece of paper folded like a fan with the word A-U-S-T-R-A-L-I-A written on it. I told Jean I had been offered an MD's job and slowly unfolded it. "AUSTRIA!" she shouted in delight! "I can use my German." Oh dear. After the shock she okayed the idea of moving to Australia, which was fortunate as we had only four weeks to hand over our jobs, pack up our sparse belongings, sell her car, obtain our visas and say "see you later" to the family.

And that was how the next adventure started. I was forty-six, Jean was thirty-nine, and we were off to Sydney for three years. But the adventure lasted for three decades and will get several chapters of its own.

SECTION TWO:
CAME FOR THREE YEARS,
STAYED FOR THIRTY

12. G'day

I'M standing in front of a tall blond man of around thirty dressed in a light-brown shirt and shorts with long white socks.

"Good morning, Mr Hampton," he says. "I see you're here on a three-year work visa. Welcome to Australia and we hope you enjoy your stay."

Stamp on passport.

Jean is next.

"G'day, Jean. See you're from America. Well you've come to another great country. You have a good time now."

Stamp.

It's the twenty-third of March, 1983, and we've arrived. Australia has just elected Bob Hawke as its new Labor Prime Minister and let us in for the Great New Adventure. All we have to do is find Margaret Townsend, my PA with the car.

We were checked in for the handover period to an apartment overlooking an inlet of Sydney Harbour, to the west of the City: a beautiful vista but convenient for nothing as we were to discover. Margaret suggested taking the rest of the day off and picking me up next morning to go to the office. The fridge was well stocked so we accepted her advice.

That was day one of a three-year sojourn that turned out lasting for thirty!

*   *   *

We had stopped en route for two days in Bangkok to meet my opposite number – Chinese, surprisingly. Thais in general hate the Chinese, but his appointment was not so surprising when you remember that this was EMI, and the British can't put up with foreigners who are racists. We also met up with my cousin

Christopher whom I hadn't seen for years, and sadly never saw again.

We crossed the Australian coastline at dawn west of Darwin and flew over the mountain ranges. I was stretching my legs at the back of the 747 when a man of about sixty joined me. He stared down at the rugged terrain.

"Look at those motherfuckers," he said. "I was all over them in forty when we were defending Oz from those fucking Japs."

I knew the Japanese never invaded Australia. Maybe he was in training down there with the Army in case they did. I didn't pursue the matter, but a bit of a discussion ensued and then I rejoined Jean, who was having a great time. She had bought a big book for touring Australia and was following our route south, pointing out the great splashes of red and yellow, like spilled paint over the desert floor, to the other passengers.

*   *   *

My first day at work was a bit like a Royal Tour.

To start with, I met the senior staff plus the outgoing MD, Peter Jamieson, whom I knew slightly and who, by another of life's amazing coincidences, had also been at Eastbourne College, though later than me. Then a visit to the junior managers and staff and a look at the recording studios. I was impressed by everyone's friendliness and noted the wide range of nationalities: New Zealanders (lots of them!), British, Chinese, and several like Alex Coroneos, the sales director, whose names indicated a European heritage. I was also taken to see the managing director of Thorn EMI, John Slater, a Yorkshireman I had met briefly in London, and his staff who occupied a small suite in the EMI building.

A chat with Peter, an hour or so with the finance director, Peter Matthews (a Kiwi), and then it was lunchtime, after which I was driven to our music publishing company in St Leonards, about fifteen minutes from EMI's HQ at 301 Castlereagh Street in the city. This visit was a curly one: the longstanding publishing boss had been fired by Peter a few weeks ago and his replacement had not yet arrived. Added to which there was some controversy over his selection. When asked by Ken East who the shortlisted candidates were, Peter replied that one was a well-known young publisher, another was the finance director at Polygram, and the third was an ex-radio man – a DJ.

"Well either of the first two," Ken declared.

"Actually, we've appointed the DJ," said Peter.

For some time I harboured the malign suspicion that Peter had engineered this situation to make things difficult for me. I never entirely lost the suspicion, but his DJ was an inspired choice and that was how Barry Chapman entered my life.

Day two, time to visit Homebush. An industrial site on the road to Parramatta beside the railway line housed our factory, printing works and distribution centre, along with the accounts and payroll departments. Past experience enabled me to chat reasonably knowledgeably with the men handling the presses and the women in the cassette plant. The distribution centre was enormous and much of the space under-utilised, but the handling methods seemed up to date and the senior management – a mixture of dinky-di Aussies and Lebanese – were cordial and ready to talk. They seemed pleased that their new MD was taking such an interest in what they were doing.

But for me the highlight was the visit to payroll.

"Ladies and gentlemen," said the director of HR who was showing me around, "may I introduce you to our new MD, Mr Nick Hampton."

At which a tall, middle-aged woman stood up, put out her hand and walked towards me.

"Me name's Shirl. How do you like to be called then, Nick?"

"Nick is good for me, Shirl, and good to meet you," I said, shaking her hand.

No time for hesitation at a moment like that.

*   *   *

And so I got to grips with my new situation. I was running an international company with over six hundred employees as well as having management oversight of the New Zealand operation, which had its own MD and another hundred staff. In terms of profit contribution to EMI Music, Australasia had often been one of the highest regions in the world, so I had quite a responsibility.

I invited myself to all the meetings for the first few weeks so I could get to know the issues and, more importantly, which of my managers was dealing with them. Scheduling new releases, production, marketing and promotion, sales, you name it and I was there. I also took the first available opportunity of visiting the four EMI branches in other capital cities.

Peter Jamieson wanted a farewell tour, which seemed in danger of lasting for weeks, and he was in no hurry to move out of the company house in St Ives which we were to occupy. Two social occasions gave me a pretty clear idea of where he was at.

The first was a dinner party in Melbourne that he organised for our local team plus the founders and owners, Michael Gudinski and Ray Evans, and senior staff of Mushroom Records, an independent label we distributed: about sixteen people in all. It was an enjoyable and very interesting experience, meeting the people behind the second biggest independent record and music publishing business in Australia. At the end of the evening PJ suggested a game of "spoof" to decide who would pay the not inconsiderable bill. Everyone appeared to agree, but Gudinski lost and stormed out of the restaurant. PJ fulminated about "bad sportsmanship" . . . and I got the bill settled. A direct insight into two monster egos.

If we needed more proof of the size of Peter's ego it came with another farewell he conveniently arranged at our house. He invited all the Old Eastbournians in Sydney, about twenty, ostensibly to introduce them to me. But in fact they were there to celebrate his birthday on the fourth of April, another party EMI paid for. I later learned that this was Peter's normal practice.

*　　　*　　　*

The record industry in Australia was in an interesting state of change in 1983, with three of the "majors" being run by expats. Polygram had the South African Bruce Mackenzie; the Aussie at

CBS was about to be replaced by an American, Bob Jamieson; and there I was at EMI. Australians were still in charge at WEA, Paul Turner, and RCA, Brian Smith. The largest "indie" label was Festival Records where the MD was Alan Hely, supported by general manager Jim White.

The six of us formed the boards of the newly founded Australian Record Industry Association (ARIA) and the Public Performance Corporation of Australia (PPCA), which were the policy-making and controlling elements of the record industry for the nation. Part of ARIA's mandate was to maintain visibility in Canberra and lobby politicians and the bureaucracy when necessary.

Alan took it upon himself to explain every nuance of the business to the newcomers. It was a thoughtful thing to do, but you could see the eye-rolling of the other locals at the first few of my monthly meetings.

*　　*　　*

I was on a lot of boards. One of the most interesting was the Australasian Performing Right Association, which came to play a huge role in our lives.

APRA, formed in 1926 when radio started to become a major user of recorded music, represents music publishers and composers and has always had a board made up of six directors from each constituency. Normally the MD of EMI's music publishing arm would automatically be elected, but as there was some controversy over Barry Chapman's appointment I was invited to take up the spare seat for the time being. This invitation was also controversial because some of the other publishers did not want a "record man" on the board. But the late and great Ted Albert pointed out that he also ran both a record and a publishing business. Ted and I became good friends and he remains one of the most interesting people I ever met. There'll be more of the remarkable and influential Albert family later.

Several of the songwriter directors would figure prominently in our lives over the next span of years. They included Glenn

Shorrock, who had recently left the Little River Band, for whom he co-wrote several hits. One, *Cool Change*, would later be voted as one of the Top 30 Australian songs in a landmark music industry poll. As LRB were on the EMI label and still selling well, we saw a lot of each other and I always found Glenn really good to deal with.

Another of the directors representing the composers was Dorothy Dodd, who also became a firm friend. She owed her fame to writing the best-known English lyrics to *Granada*, a standard which had been recorded by just about every top male singer since the Mexican Agustin Lara wrote it in 1932. What Dorothy most loved doing was sitting down at the piano and singing like Cole Porter. Later in our relationship she would ring me up and sing her own new words – very explicit ones too! – to *Let's Do It*.

Bruce Smeaton had written the scores for several successful films including *Picnic at Hanging Rock*, but he was not noted at that time for his conversation. At board meetings he sat next to me and doodled.

Ray Columbus represented the New Zealanders, who could elect one composer member to the board. He was the lead singer for a band called The Invaders who had a huge hit back in 1964, *She's A Mod*, written to typify what was happening in London that year. Ray was a funny guy who whistled a lot.

Our chairman was Robert Hughes, a delightful, supportive and genial composer of classical music from Adelaide. At the meetings, where fifteen people were present, he sat in the middle seat opposite the managing director of APRA, John Sturman. They would often lean forward over the table with their heads almost touching as if they were having a private conversation.

I learned a lot about how and how not to run a meeting in those days. And I knew those directors were bound to be a lot of fun.

*   *   *

At last Peter Jamieson left Sydney together with his wife and daughter, leaving behind their cat, his company car, and enough problems to keep me busy for the next two-and-a-half years.

*   *   *

"Mate, he's raped your catalogue."

Jim White, GM at Festival, was on the phone. We were discussing the popular *TV Compilations* LPs which had become one of the largest contributors to EMI's bottom line for the past two years. Every three months EMI, RCA and Festival joined forces to put out a "Best Of" compilation featuring their twenty best-selling singles. They competed with Polygram, WEA and CBS, who did the same thing.

In addition, EMI, under the leadership of Peter Jamieson, had put together its own "Best Of" for just about every successful artist or band on its international and local rosters, and this had provided a very large proportion of turnover and profits.

But Jim was right. Jamieson had allowed so much of our product to be used on these *TV Compilations* that there wasn't much left in the kitty.

EMI had just appointed Peter Dawkins and his offsider Peter Karpin to head up A&R, two good operators who'd enjoyed a good reputation for finding new talent for CBS, so we were hopeful that they could fill the product gap, which would however take some time.

Fortunately, a significant part of EMI's profits continued to derive from the manufacturing and distribution deals we had with Mushroom Records and Alberts.

Mushroom had several big signings including the New Zealand band Split Enz, headed up by its founder Tim Finn who was later joined by his brother Neil.

Alberts kept coming up with hits by several bands, none bigger than AC/DC whose 1980 classic *Back In Black* remains one of the highest selling albums ever released at fifty million copies. AC/DC are of course in the all-time top ten in world record sales. In their lifespan of over forty years, they have played a monumental part in establishing Australia as a breeding ground for new English-speaking talent. While AC/DC were headed up by Malcolm and Angus Young, the band's long road to the top owed much to the

82

deft navigation of their older brother George and Harry Vanda, the studio magicians who themselves came out of the biggest band of the 1960s in Australia, The Easybeats.

Another great outfit produced by Vanda and Young was Rose Tattoo, fronted by the visually alarming but utterly delightful Angry Anderson. Tattooed on all visible parts of his body, Angry is a person whom once met you will never forget. Immensely generous with his time, he helped me enormously in years to come.

Harry and George also wrote and produced *Love Is in the Air*, the John Paul Young mega-hit that has been covered by dozens of singers worldwide. It was released in the late '70s and we were still selling heaps when I got to breathe the Sydney air.

The incomparable Vanda and Young partnership, coupled with the insurance of being the second son of one of Sydney's wealthiest families, made it possible for Ted Albert to take all sorts of gambles on artists, most of which were highly successful. And although he had an excellent general manager in Fifa Riccobono who looked after day-to-day business, Ted liked to keep in touch. I was frequently invited to his recording studio in central downtown Sydney where I met all of these stars at one time or another.

With top-rank artists on third-party labels churning out plenty of hits in Australasia, our sales of records and cassettes in 1983 were encouragingly healthy. The problem was in the bottom line, as EMI kept only a relatively small percentage from these sales compared with sales of its own artists.

*   *   *

The World Record Club in Australia was another EMI subsidiary and it was floundering. Based in Melbourne – don't ask me why – this was one of the last of the record clubs that had been so popular in the '50s and '60s. Now sales were disappearing, stocks were huge and the bottom line all negative. To make matters worse, one of Jamieson's parting shots was to appoint his general manager, Brian Harris, to run it. He was loudly pissed off about being shunted down to Melbourne and took little interest in trying to sort out a solution for the club.

My job description also included overseeing the activities of EMI New Zealand which was run by David Snell. Our proficient brothers across the Tasman looked after manufacturing, sales, distribution, retail, and even had their own *profitable* record club. Ah, New Zealand, God bless it.

I had met David several times at conferences in the USA and London and we hit it off, probably because of our totally dissimilar characters and capabilities. He was practical, down-to-earth and forceful. Don't know what that says about me.

*   *   *

By June of '83 I had my head around what I was trying to achieve and the resources to help me. There were a few key managers I could rely on, by far the most important and best qualified being Nigel Wake, another Englishman, who was responsible for manufacturing, distribution and the recording studio. Nigel became a close friend and later on a partner in acquiring a yacht.

Sitting near my office was a young man who studied law in his spare time (and did qualify as a solicitor), Randall Harper. He was our director of business affairs, and I saw quickly that I could rely on his judgement. Equally important, he was "one of the lads" and had his ear to the ground. An MD needs that kind of input.

Alex Coroneos became one of my closest friends. He came up through the sales ranks and was a great staff motivator, invariably enthusiastic. We didn't always agree, but Alex was our reliable front line with the retailers – there were more than two thousand outlets in Australia in those days – and he got on well with everybody.

*   *   *

Fortunately I have always liked meeting people, because in those first months they came out of the woodwork. Retailers, recording artists and managers, concert promoters, radio and TV presenters . . . and bloody celebrities. It went on and on.

Jean and I were invited to a box at the Sydney Cricket Ground for a game of football – rugby league I think – and only one person was there when we arrived.

"Hello," I said. "I'm Nick Hampton from EMI."

"I'm in a country practice," came the reply.

"Oh, are you a doctor or a vet?" I asked.

Good one, Nick. He was the star of one of Australia's top-rating TV series, *A Country Practice*, and like so many celebs, expected to be recognised.

You could never say that about these two terrific people we met, Slim Dusty and Joy McKean. In the 1980s you would have come from another planet – or at least another continent – not to have heard of Slim, Australia's best-known and best-selling country artist. Originally signed to the Regal Zonophone label, Slim went on to sell seven million singles, LPs, cassettes and CDs in his incomparable career at EMI, making more than one hundred albums. As John O'Donnell, a later managing director, declared, Slim was a national hero and the rock upon which EMI Australia was built.

In May 1983, Slim gained something like his twentieth gold disc, which I presented at a reception in Chinatown. The press and radio were there and my cousin Sally, listening in Melbourne, heard me being interviewed and contacted me. (They always said I had a great face for radio.) We had some memorable trips with Slim and Joy, and I'll get to them. They also happened to live around the corner from us in St Ives, as did their manager Kevin Ritchie and his wife Betty. We all became good friends and dined and partied together often.

It was through Kevin that we were introduced to the gay set flourishing in the Sydney music business. They were mostly nice young men who seemed to find us fully acceptable, and we had social and business connections with many of them.

We were settling into what became a very agreeable lifestyle, with long days but lots of entertainment, travel throughout

Australia and New Zealand, as well as flights to Europe and America which helped to keep us in touch with our families.

Before there was time to look at the calendar nine months had flown by and it was Christmas 1983. We were into a whirl of work parties and socialising in St Ives, where we had formed a friendly relationship with our next-door neighbours, the Rapps.

One episode around this time gave me cause to ponder the sanity of Peter Dawkins, our head of A&R. Bhaskar Menon was in town and we took him out to lunch in Kings Cross. We were hardly seated before Peter started on a tirade. He told Bhaskar that he had made a terrible mistake appointing me as MD and that Bhaskar should have chosen him instead. He then went on to slag the A&R department – in particular its manager – at Capitol. We didn't linger over our meals. I was ropeable, but as usual, Menon let it slide and avoided a confrontation.

Then it was back to party time, which went on practically non-stop until Australia Day, the twenty-sixth of January, 1984.

13. Party Time . . . and A Bit of A Tour

ONE of our duties was to hold parties for visiting VIPs and the house in St Ives was good for that, with a large terrace near the pool and two reception rooms indoors.

Visitors preferred to come in the summer and we could cope with up to a hundred guests. Jean planned the menus and did the buying and most of the preparation, but her real stroke of genius was discovering the Ryde School of Catering, which obligingly recommended its senior students as cooks and waiters. Depending on the size of the party we would hire three or four young people to do the meeting and greeting and serve the drinks and food. Malcolm and Martin were Jean's favourites and they became her regulars.

The party we threw for Bhaskar Menon was a bit of a standout. We warned the neighbours that it was on, but even we were surprised at the number of limousines parked with their chauffeurs well into the early hours of the next morning. All the crowned heads of Sydney showbiz were at that one and Bhaskar was in his element with a captive audience.

A year later, while visiting Sydney, Ken East said he wanted to have a party and his wife Dolly rang Margaret Townsend to discuss the guest list. She recognised most of the names except one. It sounded like "Justine at Warners", but when she called up the person answering said there was nobody of that name. Further enquiries elicited that there was a man in Warners' marketing department named Des Steen, and Margaret's mis-name stuck to him for years. He was gay too, as were most of Dolly and Ken's friends. In fact the eventual guest list contained the names of practically every prominent queen in Sydney, including one broadcaster who arrived after a tiff with his boyfriend, with mascara running down his face. Several big media names were there, including the definitely not gay radio star John Laws, who became known as the "Golden Microphone" because he had one, and a guy who became head of the Federation of Australian Radio Broadcasters after managing 2SM, Gavin Rutherford.

Another big party at St Ives was the one we invited just about everyone from the Opera House to: directors, staff, supporters, benefactors and hangers-on crowded in. The manager of the EMI classical catalogue, Trish Byrne, always did a fantastic job in ensuring that EMI was invited to all the major events at the Opera House, so we had the privilege of entertaining such notables as Paul Tortellier, Neville Marriner and Klaus Tennstedt. Trish was now transferring to London and this party was a "thank you" to her. My best memory of it was the late arrival of Australia's most important conductor, who had been working that evening, with his white tie and tails slung over his shoulder. Jean and Martin greeted him at the door, saying "Good evening. You must either be from the dry cleaners or Sir Charles Mackerras."

There was no pandering to rank in Australia and I loved it.

*   *   *

Australia has a land mass about eighty per cent the size of the United States and a population of less than ten per cent. It's big and it's pretty empty, so getting about mostly involves air travel.

Our earliest trips were to the other state capitals, Melbourne, Perth, Adelaide and then Brisbane. In 1983, the term "provincial" would have overstated their dynamics. Except for Melbourne they were less exciting than Tunbridge Wells, although Perth was on the beautiful Indian Ocean and had lovely countryside. They all changed enormously, as did Sydney, in the next twenty years.

My deal with EMI allowed me to bring the children out once a year, and in August 1983, the middle of winter, Juliet and Lucy arrived. On advice from Slim and Joy, Jean and I decided on a week at Mission Beach in Far North Queensland, which was still enjoying weather warm enough to make the getaway worthwhile – especially the boat trip out to the Great Barrier Reef where we swam and snorkelled. Next year Lucy came out with her friend

Katie and the four of us had one of the most memorable trips of my life.

It began by joining Slim and Joy and other colleagues in Mount Isa for the premiere of *The Slim Dusty Movie*, which dramatised Slim's early life and career, interspersed with footage and songs from a round-Australia tour by his family.

These were the good old days when the Australian film industry was strongly supported by the Federal Government – think of *Mad Max*, *Crocodile Dundee* and *Picnic at Hanging Rock* – in the form of a tax deduction of one hundred and ten per cent for investors. I had little difficulty in persuading Thorn EMI to finance the film, which was made quickly and under budget. So far so good, but one of the government's demands, in return for the tax break, was that the film had to be screened at least once in a public cinema. The major chains laughed as they said "no thanks", and even the art houses turned *The Slim Dusty Movie* down. Country music was just not cool in urban Australia. Then some bright spark thought of Mount Isa and the premiere was scheduled for August.

No problem getting an audience, right? "The Isa" is in the middle of the desert, only nine hundred kilometres west of Townsville, "the big smoke". However, there were thousands of Aboriginals in the region and all the Aboriginals adored Slim, who also had legions of fans in the white community, like the mineworkers, so a full house was guaranteed.

A quick word about Mount Isa – founded in 1923 shortly after huge deposits of valuable minerals were discovered. It still has one of the biggest deposits of lead, silver, copper and zinc in the world, but the lead has caused health problems, most notably I think among children. Mount Isa has also produced some notable sportsmen, including the golfer Greg Norman and the tennis player Pat Rafter. Today its population is around twenty-two thousand – and it's still a bloody long way from anywhere!

The Slim Dusty Movie duly had a showing – in fact its premiere – on the tenth of August, 1984, an historic evening for outback Queensland. Admittedly it wasn't the most riveting piece of cinema, but EMI had co-financed the production and qualified for the tax break. The girls slept through it, and afterwards we all went over the road – ankle-deep in empty beer cans and broken bottles – to celebrate at a pub where we were putting on a party.

Getting the girls to sleep back at the motel was hard as our rooms were inhabited by the largest cockroaches you've ever seen. I swear you could hear them talking!

Next day was the opening of the annual Mount Isa rodeo, by who else but Slim? We had VIP seats at what was then the biggest rodeo in the southern hemisphere.

We flew from Mount Isa to Alice Springs, another amazing place. Situated to the north of the MacDonnell Ranges and straddling the normally dried-up Todd River, "the Alice" was founded in 1872 as a staging post for the telegraph system between Adelaide and Darwin. It still has many of the original buildings, and a population of around twenty thousand, including descendants of the various Aboriginal tribes that can claim forty thousand years of affinity to the land. It is now mostly given over to tourism, but also houses several hundred Americans and Australians employed at the top-secret Pine Gap tracking station.

We hired a moke and let the girls drive it in the Todd riverbed and I have an impressive photo of Katie trying to run me down. They also practised "synchronised swimming" in the hotel's freezing pool (the temperature went from a high of thirty-two Celsius to minus two in a day). We went to the Aboriginal art shops in the town, walked in the narrow canyons out in the mountain ranges, saw wallabies and kangaroos, and had one of the best – according to Jean – Mexican dinners ever at a restaurant owned by a couple of ex-United States Air Force personnel. It was such a memorable experience, with more to come.

From Alice Springs we continued on to Ayers Rock, some four hundred and fifty kilometres south-west by coach. We passed dingoes and more wallabies, but the most impressive thing was the complete lack of any distinguishing feature in the landscape until we saw a solitary mound of red rock rising nearly four hundred metres above the desert floor. In 1984, Uluru, "The Rock", had not been handed back as a sacred site to the local people and tourists were not – as they are now – banned from making the climb to the top, almost one kilometre. And that's what we did the next morning, except Lucy. She quit at the outcrop called "Chicken Rock", and I must admit I didn't blame her by the time we reached the summit. It's windy way up there and the sides of the rock slope right away from you.

We stayed in a hostel which had separate bedrooms and one big dining-cum-recreation room. In the evening we were taken to the best spot for photographing the rock in the sunset, an image I shall never forget.

Next day we went to the Olgas which, in a different way, are equally memorable. There are more than thirty soaring rock domes spread out over a large expanse of desert and one can wander amongst them through narrow gorges. Again it was windy, and in a way a little scary.

Then we took the coach back to Alice Springs and returned to Sydney. I hope the girls enjoyed it. For me it would have to be in the top three or four travel experiences of my life.

*   *   *

In my two and a half years at EMI in Australia, Jean and I tried to visit as much of this vast continent and both the North and South Islands of New Zealand as possible. We figured that once we went back to Europe we would probably never get another opportunity to explore these southlands. How wrong we were!

New Zealand and its inhabitants are an odd bunch, and Aussie piss-take jokes about the sheep population abounded. *"Which Kiwi has a thousand lovers? A shepherd."* But as football followers know, one thing they are respected for universally is RUGBY, through decades of dominance by the mighty All Blacks.

In 1983, EMI had its New Zealand office and factory in the Hutt Valley just outside Wellington. As I've mentioned, the Kiwis ran a successful operation that covered the full industry spectrum: A&R, a recording studio (also available to third parties), manufacturing and distribution, retail and a record club. The very capable managing director, David Snell, had good staff around him, including Lachie Rutherford, who went on to senior roles in

Hong Kong for WEA. At least twice a year I went to Wellington for board meetings, and I have fond memories of one big conference attended by the senior management from both Australia and NZ at Queenstown, a beautiful spot cradled between lakes and mountains in the middle of the South Island.

You could never tire of seeing so many spectacular destinations throughout New Zealand and Australia. Much later during our odyssey in Oz we came to love and frequently visit Sunshine Beach, which is on a sheltered bay just below Noosa National Park in Queensland.

We were blessed to find such fascination and natural beauty in these two great countries.

14. Back to Business

ONE of the characters I met during those first months in Sydney was Ross Turnbull, a lawyer who lived in a grand house in Mosman.

Ross had played rugby, and implied that he turned out for the Wallabies a few times, but it was just one test match against Ireland. Yet he had been elected to a Trusteeship of the hallowed Sydney Cricket Ground, where he seemed to be the unofficial doyen of the rugger set. It was in the Trustees' dining room over lunch where I first met Sir Nicholas Shehadie, their chairman, who was a Lord Mayor of Sydney as well as a former skipper of the Wallabies, with thirty test appearances to his credit. I was to meet his wife, Marie Bashir, much later when she played a very significant role in my life.

Also at that lunch was Alan Jones, who had just finished a stint as speechwriter to the previous Prime Minister, Malcolm Fraser, and was trying to secure the position as the Wallabies' coach. He seemed to me to have few qualifications for the job except an ego the size of Everest and a mouth to match. But in fairness, he did put together an outstanding team which went to Europe and came back undefeated in 1984, and later hosted the top-rating program on the talkback radio station 2GB. I must add that Sir Nicholas did not seem that impressed by him either.

The lunch party included Daryl Haberecht, a former Wallaby coach famous for his (very quickly banned!) "ball up the jumper" tactic and latterly a CBS employee who had, with Turnbull, acquired the CBS record club. They were set on opening discussions with me about taking over our record club – they were keen to buy and I was keen to sell.

After attending that lunch Jean and I were heavily wooed by Ross and Daryl. There were luncheons and matches at the SCG, parties at their homes, visits to the World Record Club in Melbourne, and ongoing discussions about the viability of the record club concept. We agreed that Australia was too small to support two such similar operations, and I said that, in principle, EMI would be happy to be out. Ross was by this time president of the Australian Rugby Union, a well-known and sought-after personality, and therefore welcome at Thorn EMI events.

Everyone seemed willing for negotiations to continue, so we started getting down to detail. The two World Record Club assets held by EMI were the membership mailing list and the stock. I wanted to transfer the lot for a nominal value, but neither EMI Music management nor the Thorn EMI board were prepared to take a significant loss, despite the record club haemorrhaging. Besides, the Turnbull/Haberecht team seemed willing and able to raise the funds for an acquisition, so during 1984 we agreed on a figure and a date and the deal was signed off.

I had made a major mistake. The deal called for half the purchase price to be paid on acquisition, with the other half deferred for nine months. I should have been more forceful with my masters and insisted on accepting a lower figure paid in total upfront. When we neared the second payment date the purchasers, who were probably not reaching their revenue forecasts, claimed that they had been fed misleading information about the World Record Club and specifically claimed that I was responsible. Legal action was threatened, and although the threats were never carried through it put the wind up the board of Thorn EMI in Australia. We never received the second instalment, and while we are not talking about a huge sum, Turnbull certainly did the dirt on me.

The cosy relationship Turnbull contrived to rip off EMI ended abruptly and I only saw him again once, about a decade later, at the finals of the International Sydney Piano Competition where he was squiring a well-known politician, Bronwyn Bishop. In between he had become CEO of the NRMA motoring organisation, which sacked him after massive overspending on expenses, and left his wife. He was rapidly heading downhill and then I heard that he was living in a refuge in the east of Sydney. It's sad, but I think Ross actually inhabited some sort of dreamworld where most of his acquaintances and family became victims to his fantasies. He died in 2015, and Daryl died after losing a lot of his own money in the World Record Club venture.

The whole affair taught me two things: firstly, if things smell too strongly of roses it's probably because someone has sprayed them with perfume; and, secondly, never, ever mix business with pleasure – at least to the extent I had with Ross Turnbull.

*　　　*　　　*

If you have a pretty important job it's not too difficult to be beguiled into thinking that it's *you* who people want to see and get to know personally, rather than the MD of EMI. I admit to sometimes being guilty of that, even though I was fully aware the job would only last for three years and then I'd be saying "farewell, friends". So sometimes it was pleasure before business for me – and I owe it to EMI for putting put me in the right place at the right time to meet some memorably fine people.

I will start with Terry Gray, who preceded Alex Coroneos as sales director before leaving EMI to start his own retail business with Terry Howard. "TG and TH" were both very well known over several years by everyone in the business for their expanding string of record shops, but when I met them they had sold their business to Palings, the music store chain.

EMI had HMV, a hugely successful subsidiary in the UK retail business, owned outlets doing well in New Zealand, and Capitol had just opened the Mister Music shops in the United States. I was told to undertake a study on the viability of EMI Music Australia setting up its own retail chain, so Alex introduced me to Terry Gray as the best placed person in Australia to give independent advice on the state of music retailing.

Our first meeting was on a sunny evening at his house overlooking the harbour towards the bridge. Terry introduced me to his wife, Kerrie, their children Julian and Kate, and we sat on their terrace, talking business and having a beer. A month or so later TG produced a report for me that explained the Australian market was solid but virtually controlled by Brashs, after buying out Palings and becoming so dominant it was difficult to see how another major competitor could survive. His conclusion was "buy Brashs or forget it".

Naturally EMI and Bhaskar Menon weren't about to accept that kind of defeatist nonsense, so in early '84, accompanied by David Snell and Graham Wong, the NZ retail manager, plus Jean, I headed off to Houston where Mister Music was headquartered.

Before I pick up the story in the USA, I want to declare that this episode introduced us to a lovely couple who became probably our best friends for over thirty years. We spent lots of weekends with Terry and Kerrie at Blackheath and Wentworth Falls and stayed in their houses in Mosman and Manly. Most importantly, our deep and mutually sustaining relationship continues even though Kerrie has passed away.

*   *   *

The trip to Houston and then Los Angeles was beautifully timed. I had never met Jean's mother, father or middle sister and here was the opportunity. We were there for work – if looking into a few record shops and talking to the CEO of Mister Music could be called work – and we also had part of a weekend to meet the Panther family.

We were met at the airport by one of the young men who ran the shops, driving a pickup with not one but two rifles in a gun rack behind his head and in easy reach. Welcome to Texas!

We were staying at a hotel outside the city and next morning Jean took a taxi to see her parents while the three of us went to the first Mister Music shop. All three shops we visited that day were similar. It was a good idea to be in a major shopping centre – there was hardly any retail business downtown – but tucked away on the third floor with no proper signage? I didn't know much about retail, but I knew you needed to be in an area with a high level of foot traffic.

The record shops were small, catering mainly for customers looking for charting material and nostalgia, mostly of the

American variety. Nothing wrong with that, I liked Sinatra too, but the selection did seem a bit limiting. Surprisingly, the sales figures weren't bad for a new venture, but David and Graham were quietly appalled because the Houston venture was not part of any grand masterplan we could discern – just a whim that some local businessmen had managed to talk someone at Capitol into backing.

I enjoyed the Sunday, lunching at Dickens Road with Jean's parents, Bill and Mary, and her sister Rosemary. Seeing that I was a married man living with their daughter, they were incredibly welcoming and we all got on. Bill was very funny but not too well and, sadly for me, it was the only time I met him.

The next day it was on to Los Angeles where we hired a car and asked Jean to chauffeur us – she was the only one who had driven in the United States before. We found our hotel, the Universal. I had been there previously in my travels with Stephen James and shared the pool with Telly Savalas, better known as Kojak of TV fame, a genuine celebrity. He was a regular at the pool as his mother had a suite in the hotel.

Like all our visits to Capitol, everyone we met from Bhaskar down was utterly charming but only interested in their own ideas. We talked about retailing and left. Back in Australia, I wrote up a report for the local board, plus Ken East in London and Bhaskar in LA. EMI's interest in record retailing in Australia was quietly forgotten, and Capitol disposed of their holding in Mister Music not much later.

*　　*　　*

Campbell Hogg – better known as Hoggo – was introduced by Tony Todman; both played rugby for Harlequins, a London club, in earlier days. Now Hoggo owned and ran the Australian licence for Linguaphone, which was still a popular way of learning a second language. He was a short, thick-set New Zealander who loved sports and had friends all over the rugby-playing world. Hoggo introduced me to the Royal Sydney Yacht Squadron and by August I was a member. I still remember the initiation ceremony.

The RSYS is one of the most prestigious clubs in Australia, enjoying a magnificent clubhouse and marina in Kirribilli. It was a huge honour for me to be invited into its membership. I met interesting people, enjoyed marvellous food, and Jean and I often stayed in its old-fashioned bedrooms after a late night out in the city. The chief stewards were wonderfully discreet. Once I was lunching quite legitimately with a much younger and rather beautiful woman when Wayne sidled up to me and whispered, "I thought you might like to know that Mrs Hampton is just checking in at reception, sir."

Leaving the RSYS nearly thirty years later was one of the saddest of moments for me.

*   *   *

Nigel Wake and I knew early on that we could rely on each other, and Jean and I also got on well with his wife, Marion, and their two teenage sons. As the technical director at EMI in Sydney, Nigel had a lot of responsibilities. But he was trained at the BBC and had the practical skills to be familiar with recording studios.

One of the best things he did was hiring Martin Benge, who was by coincidence the son of one of my old travelling companions in the Bexhill days, as studio manager, and within a year Studios 301 had been refurbished into the most sophisticated recording studio in the southern hemisphere, bringing to us big names including David Bowie and Duran Duran.

Nigel was mad on sailing and by late 1983 he and I were partners in the *Alpha Centauri*, a forty-four-foot yacht. She was sturdy and sat high in the water and was hand-built in Sweden by the man who sailed her solo to Australia via the South Pacific. That epic lonely voyage either left him bored rigid with sailing or short of money because he sold her pretty cheaply. On the down side, *Alpha Centauri* was under-equipped so Nigel undertook to do a fitout.

My election to membership of the RSYS gave us access to a mooring at Pittwater, a beautiful estuary north of Sydney, and for a wonderful year or so we had weekends sailing, picnicking and swimming from our boat. But Jean never liked it!

However, in 1985 our Swedish yacht was to give me another one of life's unforgettable experiences.

*   *   *

Dr Richard Letts had been on the edges of our lives since we arrived in Australia, but I wouldn't take a medical problem to him.

Dick has a doctorate in musicology, is a brilliant pianist, and a career bureaucrat. When I met him he had just been appointed to head up the music board of the Australia Council, which controlled the government budget for supporting the arts. The commercial music sector could be useful to Dick, and from time to time he would reciprocate by putting a good word in the right political ear. Dr Letts became a strategic ally for an industry which frankly was regarded by the political establishment as being run by cowboys and coke-heads.

A man called Hayes was running the Australian Record Industry Association when I arrived in '83, but he disgraced himself at an EMI dinner and I insisted he quit. I'm pretty sure it was Dick Letts that put us in touch with Victoria Rubensohn, who took over the reins at ARIA and became another close personal friend. She was the daughter of a man who owned the advertising agency behind the iconic "It's Time" campaign that swept Gough Whitlam to victory at the 1972 federal election – an Australian Charles Saatchi, if you like. Victoria knew *everyone*, and a visit with her to Canberra would see a red carpet unrolled as one met ministers and senior bureaucrats, as if by magic, though it was all organised in advance of course.

I saw a lot of Victoria and was probably her most frequent companion on those trips to lobby on behalf of the music industry. She was a consummate professional, and there were several issues to be addressed. The two most important were parallel imports and sales tax.

Parallel imports were records brought into Australia, usually from the Far East, at way below local prices, and more disadvantageously, sometimes before we had the opportunity to release these discs ourselves. Added to this, sales tax was effectively an imposition on manufacture rather than ultimate sale. These two factors were having a serious effect on our industry's sales and bottom line. The problem of parallel imports was never totally resolved in my time, but the tax issue was fixed when Australia abolished sales tax in favour of the GST.

Although Dick and I clicked he didn't have much time for my fellow managing directors. Dick left the Australia Council in 1987 to join the Australian Music Centre, with which I had a series of relationships throughout our time in Australia, as we'll see later.

*   *   *

Of those other record company bosses, Jean and I became most friendly with Bruce Mackenzie at Polygram and his wife Toni, for several reasons. The four of us arrived in Australia at the same time, they also lived in St Ives, the girls hit it off, and while very different in character and outlook, Bruce and I shared a belief that the industry needed to be sorted out. We also detested bullshit.

Theoretically, we had a lot in common with Bob Jamieson at CBS and I got on well with him too, eventually tying up the groundbreaking joint distribution agreement which initiated some industry rationalisation. But our partners did not get on. Jean found Mrs J. constantly bemoaning the lack of "American cookies" and never adjusting to the Australian way of life.

The three Australian managing directors were all cordial and we still see Jim White from Festival once in a while, but generally they looked upon us expats as here today and gone tomorrow. Which we usually were.

*   *   *

Several other people from that era stick in my memory.

One is Jenny Morris, who was just starting out on her singing career when I got to Sydney. Another Kiwi, she had the talent but seemed to have difficulty in finding the right direction and, so importantly for all creative performers, the right management. She broke through in 1986 and '87 and has won many awards, as well as being very involved in the creation of the music therapy centre in Penrith, of which there'll be more later.

Jenny certainly found success when she teamed up with Neil Finn. He was a really interesting character who brought Crowded House to EMI, mostly I think because he knew and liked Peter Dawkins, a fellow Kiwi. Then Neil, not unreasonably, demanded a guaranteed release in America and Capitol insisted on an exclusive worldwide contract. EMI Records Australia was effectively reduced to the status of licensee for its own territory.

Ted Albert had helped me join the APRA board, and EMI distributed records on his own label. Ted had immense talent and entrepreneurial flair, and a golden ear for a hit song. He helped to create The Easybeats, was influential in the success of AC/DC, and put together and financed *Strictly Ballroom*, Baz Luhrmann's smash-hit movie.

Ted wasn't into bullshit either, or long lunches. One day he invited me to the studio and we shared an orange and a banana. He never mixed family and business and he was extremely hard to get to a party. It was a terrible loss for everyone who knew him and the entertainment industry he thrived in when Ted died suddenly in 1990

Since then I've met Ted's father, his two brothers, and the only male descendent of the three Albert boys, David, with whom I've had a strong relationship for many years, particularly in connection with the Nordoff-Robbins music therapy centre which he co-chaired for several years.

The Alberts are a fascinating family who have spanned six generations in the Australian music business since the 19th century. It has been a rare privilege to know and work with them.

*   *   *

So there are some of the people who helped or hindered me during my time at EMI – and I haven't got to the Thorn EMI board yet.

When Thorn merged with EMI in 1979, the Australian corporate authorities demanded a public share offer: forty per cent as I recall. When I arrived in Sydney, EMI Music was one element of a public company with disparate business interests. Two were core Thorn activities: the rental of both new televisions and radios, and other domestic electrical equipment. It's history now, but Sir Jules Thorn made a fortune – and gained his knighthood – by being the first to work out that he could make more money renting consumer products than selling them on HP (hire purchase), because there were controls on the interest rates. So he set up Radio Rentals. His second big discovery: rentals were frequently returned by customers who were after something newer, cheaper or whatever. So Sir Jules opened a second chain of shops which catered for such demand by renting out different brands of TV sets, for instance, on different terms. This often gave him two outlets in the same area that appeared to be competing with each other – and it was all perfectly legal.

In Australia the two Thorn chains were Radio Rentals and Canberra Television, and the managing director of each was on the board of Thorn EMI, as were the MDs of Thorn Defence, who allegedly made and supplied technical equipment to the armed forces. We were never allowed to ask precisely what because it was an "official secret" (more bullshit!). Also on the board was the managing director of the newly formed Thorn Video, Les Smith, who had previously worked at EMI Records where he gained the soubriquet of "Last Minute Les". He got the job because few people in EMI thought there was a future in videos. There we go again!

In 1983, this happy little bunch were under the chairmanship of Vern Lorch, a big Texan who had spent his life in the oil business – yet another inspired EMI choice, one might think, for a conglomerate of companies which mostly supplied consumer goods. But Vern was a nice guy who at least listened and made some positive contributions. He was particularly friendly to me when he met Jean, a fellow Texan.

However, when Vern retired in '84 we inherited Sir John Mason. Now if anyone ever typified the self-preserving British civil servant it was him. An undistinguished though unblemished career as a diplomat, then the obligatory knighthood and a career victory lap with a pre-retirement posting out to the colonies . . . sorry, the Commonwealth. Pip, pip, old chap, I'll have a gin and tonic! There seemed to be few other reasons for John cutting himself off from his old pals back home. Like Vern, he had no experience of consumer goods, indeed any form of commerce. In fact the only things he had ever run were committees.

The permanent staff of Thorn EMI consisted of the previously mentioned John Slater, a limp finance director and a couple of assistants, all housed one floor below me. I would get to know them all quite well.

*   *   *

Let's finish this chapter on some positive notes.

We had some great times at EMI in Australia which included visits by world-famous artists. Duran Duran came to Sydney and recorded in our studio over two or three weeks. It seemed longer, but I got used to going in and out of our building surrounded by screaming teenage girls and seeing "We love you Nick" graffitied all over the walls (gee, they hardly knew me). Duran Duran were okay, but they demanded that we guarantee the rent of a big house in the eastern suburbs. We couldn't say no because the Nick in question was Nick Rhodes, the nephew of the deputy chairman of Thorn EMI.

David Bowie recorded *China Girl* off his *Let's Dance* album in our studio. We were introduced to him before he gave a marvellous concert at the SCG. We also welcomed and entertained Cliff Richard, now Sir Cliff, on a concert tour.

Elton John used Studios 301 too. Elton of course captured worldwide media attention when he momentarily forgot himself and married Renata Blauel, a member of his recording team. It was Sydney's social event of the year in 1984.

And last, but certainly not least, there was the Queen tour. They started with a gig in Auckland, after which Freddie Mercury had a spat with the band and refused to leave his room. Our dear friend

Peter Ikin was asked to "talk him out". Queen then turned up in Sydney for a packed press conference which I chaired. Later in the week Jean and I and members of my team hosted a dinner party for the band. She sat next to Freddie and they were engrossed in their mutual love of opera and his recent recording with Montserrat Caballé, while I was with Brian May and we talked about the stars . . . in the sky. It was a marvellous way to start the hugely successful Australian leg of their tour.

15. Still Plenty Happening

1984 dawned. We had been in Australia going on ten months and were beginning to get a feel for the place.

January is the month the rural city of Tamworth in New South Wales welcomes the annual Country Music Festival of Australia. Who was the crowned king of Tamworth? Slim Dusty of course, and to be there with him and Joy was like being a longstanding senior courtier. Everyone in town was happy to meet us.

Tamworth is four hundred and five kilometres from Sydney and in January the stifling air is like a furnace, although sometimes – Australia being such an extraordinary land of weather extremes – the Peel River running through town floods at festival time.

The oppressive heat encourages the men to keep up their fluid intake and I recall the pubs opening around nine-thirty. The first bloke in my group ordered – "shouted" in Australian – ten schooners of beer and handed them around to his mates. Then someone ordered another ten, and on it went. I joined in the shout but think I only ever sank three beers.

The evening of the Golden Guitar Awards was a smasher, and that year Reg Lindsay, who was married to Joy McKean's sister, Heather, scored the Roll of Renown Award. Slim had won it a few years earlier, as did Smoky Dawson. Smoky also lived not far from us in Sydney and our paths crossed later.

We went for a drive out of town and found Ted Egan. In this part of the world properties were sometimes called "Downs" and Ted had named his "Sink A Tinny Down", which was pretty appropriate. He was singing one of his bush ballads and accompanying himself on his "Fosterphone", an empty carton of Foster's beer cans that he beat with his hand and his fingers. Ted was a great guy and we saw him a few times before he was appointed Administrator of the Northern Territory in 2003. He was a real "bushie": he loved the bush, and the bush was good to him.

If Slim was the "King" of Tamworth, in my opinion Smoky was "God". He wasn't at Tamworth that year, but we met him with Slim at another celebration of country music nearer to home. Smoky was over seventy then, but he still came in on his horse, playing his acoustic steel string guitar. He was Australia's Singing Cowboy, in the style of America's Gene Autry. Smoky never had a huge hit, but that didn't matter. He became an entertainment legend without one and he was singing right up to his death in 2007. It was a privilege to know him.

*   *   *

Another trip to the bush. John Sturman, the CEO of APRA, and his wife Zelda invited us to join them for Easter at their property at Byrock in northern NSW. First they drove us to Lightning Ridge which is famous for its black opals. We were amazed to see men going down deep holes they had dug which were not much more than a metre wide.

In the main street of Lightning Ridge we watched the annual goat race. Goats were pulling small "jockey" carts and it was everybody's job to stop them veering off course and into the crowds of spectators, who would set them upright when they hit the kerb and jettisoned their passengers. An amazing event, but I believe that it's since been stopped and I'm not really surprised.

We then set off for the Sturmans' property along a narrow dirt road until we came across a couple who said it was closed up ahead. We had to backtrack and go via Walgett and Nyngan, where we stopped at an RSL club. We were pretty tired and maybe I'd had one too many, but when the lights dimmed at six o'clock I thought it was time to celebrate someone's birthday, so I clapped and shouted "Bravo" . . . just as the PA system started playing *The Last Post* in memory of the ANZAC war dead. I wanted to curl up in embarrassment.

We finally made it to Byrock and the Sturman property, where the house was more than five kilometres from the front gate. On the way we were passed by a kangaroo well over two metres tall who bounded alongside the car and cut straight across us. I could hardly believe my eyes.

But the most amazing thing we saw on that drive was the plague of mice, pouring over the road in endless waves as hawks and other predators stood at the side of the road just looking at them after taking their fill. Even the Sturmans' house was full of mice, and if we got rid of one lot, another lot came rushing in. John gave us the only bed with metal legs, which he placed in big dishes of water to keep (most) of the mice away from us, but in the night we could hear Zelda giggling at our discomfort.

John and his dentist son, Mark, were known for their practical jokes. On the way to Byrock, John told us of a previous visitor who, in the dim light of the outside dunny, had seen a snake rearing up by the door. Too scared to spot that it was a cobra not native to Australia – and a stuffed one at that – he ran out into the sunlight trying to pull up his trousers, only to be greeted by a delighted audience. I was pretty wary of going to that loo anyway.

In the morning John was telling us about some other folks who lived in the region, including two men who disappeared some months earlier. They were thought to be drug smugglers who had maybe fallen out with the wrong people. He had many interesting stories.

Later on we went for a drive in Mark's ute. Mark and John were in the cabin, Jean and I and Mark's two dogs were standing in the tray. The ute stopped midway over a watercourse.

"Look at that," John said.

We looked down and saw it: a glistening, white, fleshless hand coming up through the mud.

"Ohmigod!" I yelled.

We got out of the ute and approached the hand. Either Jean or I gingerly touched it and pulled it out of the water: a perfect plaster of paris hand made by a dentist! That's what Aussies call a "gotcha".

Jean and I were also pillion passengers on two dirt bikes and we shot a wild boar. After enough action and excitement to last us a month of Sundays, we got home in a state of total exhaustion from the long weekend you had to be on to believe.

*   *   *

By an amazing coincidence we discovered that the songwriting married couple Tony Hatch and Jackie Trent also lived just around the corner from us in St Ives. They often took us out on Pittwater on their cruiser, *Melody Maker,* and we attended music industry events with them too, such as the APRA Awards. Tony took us once in a chauffeured white Rolls-Royce. "Make a statement" must have been his motto – or maybe it was Jackie's.

I had been a guest at their wedding reception in London. We all waited in the basement alongside a piano, and then heard *"Here they come!"* – Jackie holding up her hand for Tony to take as he walks two steps behind to avoid her flowing white bridal dress. He has to bend forward as they come down the stairs and is in danger of falling over. The pianist begins to play *The Two of Us,* and as they reach the floor Tony slides onto the stool and takes over. Jackie leans on the piano and sings . . . and does several encores. Jackie never was shy.

They were both talented, but as a songwriter Tony was in a class of his own. It was well known in the music world that several of "his" hits were later changed to "their" hits, for copyright purposes and to satisfy her ego.

*   *   *

One of the activities that kept me busy during 1984 was negotiating EMI's joint distribution deal, not only with Bob Jamieson of CBS Records but also with my own team.

Our warehouse at Homebush used to store brown goods as well as records. Now it only handled vinyl singles, EPs and LPs, and cassettes. Product ordering and processing, stock control and delivery instructions had transitioned to a mainframe computer.

Interstate orders were trucked to Sydney airport and shipped as airfreight on Ansett, Australia's second domestic airline in 1984. This distribution method was effective, timely, and popular with our sales staff and customers, but very costly. We were virtually providing an overnight delivery service to the major cities and an incredible one for smaller towns.

Bob and I agreed that the CBS catalogue could be stored and shipped out of Homebush, and that our online systems could be tweaked and jointly improved. It was further agreed in principle that his IT manager and our distribution manager would be retained and redundancies would be kept to a minimum. As there was a fairly high turnover of manual staff anyway, this should not present a problem.

We also agreed to look at the alternative of overland delivery and I checked out several trucking companies. One looked perfect and quoted a service at about one-third the cost of using Ansett. The downside was that deliveries into Victoria and Queensland would take on average an extra day, to Adelaide an extra two, and to Perth four. But New South Wales was unaffected, and as it provided over thirty per cent of our total business (compared to Western Australia with less than ten) this proposal sounded like a goer. At least to me and Bob, who had asked CBS in New York for a transfer home, so we wanted the deal wrapped up.

Our sales teams were furious! My dear friend Alex Coroneos and his mob went so far as to perform a song on stage at our annual sales conference called "Fuck Trucks". Not good publicity for me, and Slater, one of my bosses, was in the audience. Ansett sent a nasty letter to our retailers saying in effect that this bastard Hampton was going to ruin their business. Didn't I cheer when Ansett went bust in 2001! Anyway, we tabled the proposal for joint distribution and airfreight was maintained, with some savings. Our directors agreed, and the EMI/CBS joint distribution service was born.

*　　　*　　　*

On the whole, 1984 was a pretty good year for business as well as social engagements. Sales of records in Australia were holding up, with the EMI/RCA/Festival "Best Of" compilations pulling in up to 300,000 for each issue. We had stopped the losses of the World Record Club and Castle Music, the EMI publishing company, had settled down with its new MD Barry Chapman, who was now a frequent social companion with Ros, his wife at the time.

There were several international conferences to which the heads of the larger EMI companies were invited. The principal purpose as far as we could tell was to still allow the insufferable Bhaskar Menon to go on boring us to death until way past midnight. However, one conference in New York was highly notable.

Two celebrities had been invited to address us. First up, Andrew Lloyd Webber. He was, surprisingly, a speaker who failed to engage his audience. What he told us about the art of writing a musical made it sound like a science. It was more of a dry technical exposition than an intriguing insight into the creative mind of one of the greatest composers of the 20th century and his collaboration with the brilliant lyricist Tim Rice.

Then it was the turn of Sarah Brightman, his wife and the female lead in the London production of *Cats* in which she played Grizabella, one of the Jellicle cats. Not only beautiful, she had personality too. She used her skills as an actress to captivate the audience, telling us what it was like to appear in a fabulous musical and taking us inside her relationship with Andrew, what it was really like living with a genius. Sarah went on to star in Lloyd Webber's even bigger production, *The Phantom of the Opera*.

They both stayed on to mix with the audience, and this unique experience in "The Big Apple" made me even keener to see *Cats* when it came to Australia.

16. An End . . . and A New Beginning

1985 started off with another trip to Tamworth followed by a visit from my son Jerry and his girlfriend Sandy. Jean and I spent time with them on the harbour and up in Ku-ring-gai Chase, the national park between Sydney and the Hawkesbury, and the three of them waved me goodbye from a friend's cruiser as I bravely set sail for Lord Howe Island, four hundred nautical miles away.

I was part of an all-male crew on the *Alpha Centauri* that included Nigel, Steve Wagner, the finance director at WEA, and three of Nigel's acquaintances who at least had some knowledge of navigation and use of the radio – none of us had made an ocean trip in a yacht before.

There was a decent wind up and we made good time, but Nigel was seasick almost the whole way. On the third night I was awoken by the two men on watch.

"What the fuck is that?" one said.

"No fucking idea," was the reply.

Sleepily, the rest of us got up on deck and there, right in front of us, was a massive black shape climbing out of sight in the moonlight. Someone looked at a chart and worked out that it had to be Ball's Pyramid, a six hundred-metre-high volcanic remnant. The problem was we couldn't work out how close we were to running aground. Nigel and our navigator decided to change tack and give it a wide berth, so we sailed around it to the north and by daybreak we were sitting off Lord Howe Island, waiting for the harbourmaster to arrive and give us directions for coming in.

"Line yourself up on me and the big mark on the cliff," he radioed, "and keep going until I drop my arm. Then go hard to starboard."

It was a bit hairy passing within feet of wrecks that didn't make it.

The weather wasn't great, nor was Nigel. He insisted on a bed, so we left our bunks behind and checked into a lodge, quite gladly it must be said. The next couple of days we roamed the island and met the "natives", Australians whose families had mostly been there for generations, learned why the rats lived in the palm trees – originally to find food – and discovered the Lord Howe woodhen, which comes out of hiding if you clap your hands. Unsurprisingly it was on the endangered species list.

Nigel improved, though not enough to look forward to sailing home when the time came. He might have said under his breath Lord, how? Anyway, we left the island on a high ebb tide, and even then our keel clipped the reef but we were off and away.

We roared along in a gale with the stern in the air. First Nigel got seasick again, then three of the others, leaving Steve and me – who had the least sailing experience – on deck, where we spent the next twenty-four hours taking it in turns to steer and huddle under the rail for protection from the wind.

By the third morning the wind had died down and most of the crew were back on their feet. A smudge on the horizon came into view: land-ho! But where were we exactly? Our radio had conked out and we only knew that we'd been heading in a westerly direction. As we sailed closer to the smudge we could make out an industrial skyline, which meant that we weren't near Sydney. It had to be either Newcastle or Wollongong, both steelworks cities. We gambled that it was Newcastle and turned to port to ride down the coast. We must have been born sailors after all because we had pulled the right rein, and that evening we were safely moored back in Pittwater.

It was an experience none of us shall ever forget – or repeat. For Nigel it was "Goodbye forever, *Alpha Centauri*." He immediately declared his inability to ever go to sea again, which was a shame because he had put so much effort into preparing for the trip. So the *Alpha Centauri* was back on the market, and not too long afterwards both Nigel and I left EMI. We kept in touch for a few years but he kept changing jobs and plans, took the family back to the UK, and we lost contact. Jean and I were having breakfast in Noosa some time in the mid-nineties when we received a message that Nigel had died in a hotel in Dubai. It was very sad news. The Wake family had been good friends and Nigel one of my best.

*   *   *

I was fortunate to meet two more highly talented music people in the first half of 1985.

At that year's APRA Awards the gong for "Most Performed Music For Film" went to Bruce Rowland for the soundtrack to *Phar Lap*, which was published by Castle Music. It was a very proud honour for our subsidiary to win an award and a thrill for me to meet Bruce, a lovely bloke and a great composer of film scores. I for one will never forget the opening of the 2000 Olympic Games in Sydney when a lone rider galloped into the stadium to the tune of *The Man From Snowy River*.

I also met someone else who would become a good friend and supporter when he was on the APRA board in the '80s and '90s: Eric McCusker, winner of the award for "Most Performed Popular Work" for Mondo Rock's *Come Said The Boy*.

*   *   *

Cameron Mackintosh arrived in Sydney several months before the premiere of *Cats* and took an office downtown to oversee the staging of the blockbuster at the Theatre Royal. He also wanted to make a "semi-live" recording of the show for the Australian market, and that's how I came to meet him. He was a very agreeable and enormously successful theatrical producer and he became a regular visitor to EMI Studios 301 during production of the album.

Cats opened in July and we were there on the first night with celebrities and dignitaries including Bob Hawke. It was a runaway success, going brilliantly right up to the moment Debbie Byrne was about to sing *Memory*, the showstopper – when the show really did stop. Police raced into the front stalls and hurried the Prime Minister away. Then the music cut out, the curtain came down, and a voice over the PA intoned: "Ladies and gentlemen, please leave your seats row by row starting from the front, go out of the theatre and await further instructions." There had been a bomb threat and the PM's security detail was taking it deadly seriously.

Thankfully, nothing came of it. We waited in the corridors of the shopping mall, in the same building as the theatre, for forty-five minutes. Bob Hawke reappeared and started walking around, chatting to people, which was a nice touch, and we were let back in. The person everyone felt sorry for was Debbie Byrne, who carried on like a trouper and received a huge ovation when she finished her fabulous song.

*   *   *

Board meetings! What a curse. What a drag. Set aside a day at least. The board demanded frequent detailed reports both oral and in writing, and it soon became clear that the MO of Mason and Slater was to pick on one of the managing directors and harass him, meeting after meeting. The first one they picked on was the MD of Canberra TV, and they managed to dislodge him within twelve months

The second one in their sights was me.

Trying to explain that sales were below budget because a major international release was delayed was a waste of time; clearly we should be expected to have another monster album in the pipeline. No brussel sprouts? Well sell cauliflowers instead.

I had a break in August and went back to London to see the kids and confer with my colleagues at EMI Music in Gloucester Place. They confirmed what I was seeing and hearing in Australia. Few of the EMI Music staff had any time for Ken East. He wouldn't stand up to Bhaskar, but he didn't mind bullying the juniors.

Capitol was as introverted as ever, frustratingly difficult to deal with. They didn't want to release EMI product even if it was charting in its home country. There was a story circulating that the Thorn EMI top brass wanted to see Bhaskar pushed out, but they couldn't admit to shareholders that firing him would trigger a five million-dollar severance payout, an enormous sum in those days. He kept his job and now enjoys a bloody huge pension.

On top of that, Thorn EMI was still locked in a stupid struggle with Philips over the use of the compact disc which Philips had patented and first produced in 1982. Philips said other companies could use this revolutionary format in return for paying a small royalty on each CD pressed. By mid-1985, nearly every major record company in the world had agreed, but EMI held out and was excluded from the fast-growing CD market. It was another extraordinarily dumb, inexplicable and very costly decision.

I ran into Bhaskar one morning in the foyer of the Southern Cross Hotel in London. The windbag was unusually uncommunicative and cool towards me. I found out later that in my absence Peter Dawkins, my unstable A&R director, had written a letter to *Billboard*, the international music magazine produced in the USA, that was scathing of Capitol and its A&R team in particular. Thanks Peter.

By the time I got back to Australia I was fed up and almost looking forward to returning to EMI Music in London after my three-year tenure in Sydney, although it was unclear what I would be doing there. But in September that option was removed. I was called into the office of John Slater, who was accompanied by an unexpected face: Ken East.

Without much preamble they fired me on the spot. No compensation, no job offer in London, just "Be out by next Tuesday and on a plane." I was escorted from the building as if I had been found guilty of fraud or rape. To say I was in shock would have been an understatement.

*   *   *

That was the end of nearly eight years with EMI. On the whole it was a great experience, with so many opportunities to travel and meet people, but disappointing to rediscover that hard work and loyalty so often go unrewarded.

Getting sacked, however, was probably one of the best things that happened to me in my whole working life as it opened up so many new doors.

The next morning I followed up a phone call from a journalist friend, Phil Tripp, and went to his office in Chinatown. He had heard the news and knew that Rupert Perry was coming in from EMI Records to replace me.

"Do you want to stay in Australia?" he asked. I pointed out the difficulties which included no job, no long-term visa, no home and not much money.

"Let's see if we can do anything about your being able to stay, first of all. I want you to meet a mate in this building and we can do that right now. I've made an appointment. He's a solicitor, his name is Gerard Craddock, but he's known as Crash. Let's go."

Crash shared an office with Terry Buddin. We walked in and sat down. The first thing I noticed was the filing cabinet behind him labelled "Crash Victims".

"Yes," Crash said, "those are my client files. I deal exclusively with criminals and illegal immigrants and really there's not much difference between them in the eyes of the law. But what are you?"

After my explanation Crash said he would speak off the record with a pal in the Immigration Department and get back to me straight away. He was very interested to hear that Rupert Perry was being shipped in and reasonably confident that my visa would be valid for the remaining five months of my contract. He called me that afternoon and the next day Jean and I were in his office.

"Right," he said, "let's kick off with the good news. Firstly, Immigration have stuffed up. They've allowed EMI to transfer the remainder of your visa period to Perry and that is just not permitted. Visas are granted to specific people and are never transferable, so it looks to me like your ex-boss Mr Slater has spoken to his mate in the department and they've done a deal. Very naughty, but a big help to us."

I nodded and smiled.

"Secondly, you are in principle allowed to stay in Australia till your visa expires. You could always say you wanted a holiday before leaving. But you'll have to play it as it comes and I'll get back to that."

"Sure," I said, feeling encouraged.

"Thirdly," Crash continued, "I strongly recommend that you lodge an application to apply for a long-stay visa immediately. Normally you can only do that when you're not in Australia, but I think that in these circumstances you might get the right to apply while you're still here. Otherwise it means a trip to New Zealand and probably a long wait."

Jean and I looked at each other blankly.

"Now for the downside. You can't work, or at least you can't draw a salary or be officially employed. And that could be for several months even assuming you get permission to apply for the visa. And a warning: the Immigration Department can get up to some nasty tricks, like detaining people for fifteen days if it suspects they're infringing the regulations. So I recommend you do two things. Keep your passports and credit cards handy, and if you find yourselves in the back of a truck heading for the Villawood Detention Centre, suggest that everyone would be better off if the driver took you straight to the airport and put you on a plane to Auckland. You might even be grateful and drop him a bung."

Crash didn't wait for our response to his game plan. He ploughed on.

"And now you've got to get things sorted out with EMI. How about a meeting with Slater this arvo? Don't mention what we've found out about the visas, that can come as a surprise later if necessary. And make it sound as if you're getting ready to leave Australia next week. Let the bastard think he's got you on the run. Good luck and stay in touch."

*   *   *

John Slater on his own looked a lot less confident than when he was backed up by Ken East. He started to speak. I interrupted him.

117

"Thank you, but I heard enough from you two days ago," I said firmly. "Now I'll tell you what we and particularly you are going to do. If you want us out of the house and the company car back by Tuesday as you stated I suggest you give instructions for me to receive a cheque tomorrow for the following: my salary for the remaining five months of my contract, plus any holiday pay accruing up to the beginning of next March, two thousand towards the cost of freighting our furniture and belongings back to the UK, and the value of two business class tickets from Sydney to London. Failing that I shall have no recourse but to stay in the house and retain the car. Is that clear?"

Slater was gobsmacked.

"We could book the plane tickets for you?" was all he managed.

"Quite unacceptable," I replied. "I shall book the flights with whom I wish and for when I wish. And if that's all, I'll leave it with you and I'll be back at eleven-thirty tomorrow to pick up the cheque."

The cheque was ready.

We had no idea we had so many friends. The phone hardly stopped ringing, and once we were able to say that our hope was to stay in Australia we were besieged by people wanting to help. But first things first: we had to find somewhere to live.

This proved to be easier than expected. We went to a real estate agent in Mosman and picked out a house that had a spectacular view overlooking the Spit Bridge on the eastern side of Middle Harbour. We were told that one of the agent's reps was about to show it to someone else but we could catch him there if we went straight away. When we turned up he said he was expecting another couple and didn't know about us. We told him we were next in line, took a look around, quietly agreed it would suit us for a few months, and said we would take it. Done! We bolted back to his office and 14 Ida Avenue was ours, signed and sealed – as it turned out, for the next three years.

Alex Coroneos organised a team of beefy Maoris to move us, we hired a van, and on the following Tuesday we were relocated. I left the keys to the EMI house in St Ives under the mat and the company car in the garage.

One of the many calls and offers of help came from Warwick Doughty, who owned a telemarketing company with another youngish man, David Hammer. One of their main products was a record label called Telmak, which produced "soundalike" albums and compilations. I had met them a few times when they were trying to negotiate some rights with EMI. To say they were considered by the "legit" record companies to be a bit on the shady side would be an understatement, and they made no secret of the fact that they were approaching me to add a bit of class to their outfit. Well, if the cap fits wear it! I agreed to help them in negotiations for new product and oversee their financial affairs, which they certainly needed.

Jean had her own car, so the boys gave me one to use, a lovely old Mercedes. But how to pay me? Another visit to Crash, and another part of the plan was put in place. In those days an "illegal" could not be employed, but there was nothing to stop him from owning a private limited company to which fees for consultancy work could be paid. And so Direct Music Pty Ltd was born with Jean and myself as the two shareholders and directors. The company earned fees by hiring out our services and then "lent" us sufficient funds to pay our living expenses. In due course it became the ownership vehicle for our own retail and mail-order business, and more of that later.

Amazingly, within ten days we had a home, two cars, and a means of financial support. Now all we needed was that application for a permanent visa.

*   *   *

Slater must have been furious when he heard what we had done and he did everything he could to make life difficult for us. For instance, his PA had the audacity to ring up and say she just needed to "borrow" our passports. He claimed that we had taken company-owned furniture from St Ives, but I had kept all the invoices for everything we had purchased when we arrived, and at that time the house was practically bare.

The Immigration Department also asked for our passports and started threatening to send us to Villawood, but I told them to contact Crash and eventually they gave up. However, it was not pleasant.

Crash helped us to lodge the request for permission to apply for our permanent visas, and just before Christmas 1985 it was approved. But we still had to fulfill other criteria. The most essential was the offer of a permanent position from an employer who could not find a suitable local candidate. In other words, I had to prove I wasn't doing an Aussie out of a job. Again Messrs Doughty and Hammer came to the rescue: Telmak needed a chartered accountant with international experience at a high level in the music industry – and this was the killer – who could speak French. There was only one applicant and he got the job, and in 1986 he got his permanent visa and one for his partner.

A bright new life for us was starting after my sudden separation from EMI.

*　　　*　　　*

In 1984-85 we had seen the release of a few recordings on CD and I was convinced this new format would take over the market just as cassettes had done in the second half of the '60s. But hardly anyone in Australia seemed to be taking CDs seriously. Only one shop, in Adelaide, was stocking the few imports available so we decided that this was an opening for Direct Music Pty Ltd and started to search for a suitable retail site.

Chatswood was growing fast in the mid-eighties, attracting huge numbers of customers on the North Shore to its three shopping centres. Shop rentals were much cheaper here than in the city's CBD and one of the attractions of Chatswood was free parking. People could park in Chatswood Chase, which had just opened, shop, have lunch, go to the cinema, and leave their car for as long as they wished. We took a lease on 14 Anderson Street, just up from the Chase, got the shop fittings from friends of Terry Gray who manufactured them, and opened in March 1986.

The shop, run by Jean, was an overnight success and we received a lot of media attention, particularly from Radio 2GB with whom we advertised on Saturday mornings. This station was relayed nationally, so we got enquiries from all over Australia, which led to the setting up of our Compact Disc Club to handle the mail-order side of the business and send out bulletins for new releases. It also became an important source of information for the major labels, who were still importing limited quantities of CDs. At first our product range was mostly classical and jazz, often sourced via small independent importers, but as new releases of pop and rock came on stream we bought our stock through a friendly retailer in Bondi.

Soon we had accounts with all the majors including EMI, as well as the independents, and hundreds of titles on our shelves. We were becoming a popular haunt for shoppers in Chatswood, and regular customers were offered membership of the Compact Disc Club and a small discount. Later on we introduced special evenings for club members where we put out stock at reduced prices and served drinks. We were almost stopped by the police one evening over the drinks, but as we weren't *selling* alcohol we weren't breaking any licensing laws.

In 1986, Telmak was sued by CBS/Sony for "passing-off" their soundalike recordings as originals and I was asked to appear for the defence in the High Court, before a learned and bewigged judge. The CBS case was handled by David Catterns whom I had met several times during my stint at EMI, and he was the best copyright lawyer in town. He cross-examined the Telmak boys and Don Bruner, their repertoire manager, in his usual courteous but forensic manner, and one could tell from the judge's interjections that he was not leaning in Telmak's favour. I was not looking forward to my turn in the witness box.

I knew David professionally and he helped me enormously, almost putting words in my mouth, by asking me to explain several matters directly to the judge, who was so friendly I almost expected an invitation to lunch. Everyone said I helped to win the favourable verdict, namely that Telmak was only obliged to make it clear on the record sleeves and cassette covers that the recordings were soundalikes and not the originals. Both sides bore their own costs, Hammer and Doughty were delighted, but my old sparring partner at CBS, Denis Handlin, was not happy.

I helped David and Warwick in another way when I warned them off an "offer" from their over-friendly ANZ bank manager. Like many start-ups, Telmak and Demtel – another marketing company using cheap TV time to advertise – never had enough money in the till, and the boys led a pretty expensive lifestyle. They always needed to borrow, and the ANZ would be ready to lend by thinking up new ways to make a dollar without considering the risk exposure to their clients. This was the era of the "Swiss Franc Loan", whereby borrowers, for an initial fee, would get a loan in Swiss currency, converted by the bank into Australian dollars for a second profit, at interest that was less than half the going rate in Australia. Sound good? It did to the boys until I showed them what would happen if the Aussie dollar sank against the Swiss franc. Fortunately they took my advice, but thousands of other borrowers swallowed the bait and lost huge amounts in ensuing years.

By the end of '86 my "cameo" with Warwick and David was done. We parted good friends and stayed in touch. I had helped them quite a bit, they had helped us enormously, and it was time to move on to new things.

*　　　*　　　*

We were now making a handy profit from selling CDs and the next year I saw the potential in opening a second store, one in Parramatta. We leased a good site with a lot of passing foot traffic and put Caroline, a delightful young woman, in charge. She sold a lot of product to young men! In 1987, we turned over more than a million dollars, which enabled us to buy our first house in the Blue Mountains.

However, we had not foreseen the danger of our success.

All the retailers were now into CDs and the big chains, like Brashs, were using their clout to get favourable deals. Then Warner did the dirty on us by reissuing huge chunks of their back catalogue at mid-price while we still had the original full-price releases in stock. We wrote off tens of thousands of dollars and saw the red light flashing: we had to get out.

We did, though not elegantly. Some of our creditors were lenient and some not so. We put the company into liquidation. Jean was actually pleased: she hated retailing despite being so good at it.

*   *   *

We moved from Mosman to our house at Blackheath which fortunately was not financially compromised and Jean got a job as PA to the headmaster of Blue Mountains Grammar, a private co-ed school run by a Church of England trust which was chaired by the Bishop of Parramatta. Just her cup of tea.

Almost simultaneously I got a job working for Dick Letts at the Australian Music Centre in Sydney. I've mentioned Dick before because he cropped up at different times and in different ways throughout our years in Sydney.

It was an interesting job but the pay was terrible, so I was only slightly embarrassed when, after three months at the AMC, Terry Gray contacted me to ask whether I would be interested in applying for the position of CEO at the Video Industry Distributors Association. This was at a time – early 1988 – when the video rental business was huge worldwide. In Australia the industry leaders had hit on a great business model. By putting out their product on sale-or-return to the video stores, who then rented the videos to the public, they could minimise and delay their sales tax liabilities, just as we had done earlier at EMI with the TV-marketed albums.

VIDA had a staff of two, myself and my assistant, Wendy Clifford. We shared an office near Central Station with the trade association of the film industry, so the two organisations were handling virtually the same product in different forms. I commuted from the Blue Mountains by train and stuck it out at VIDA for nearly two years, but the work was undemanding and by early 1990 I was getting bored. Then the phone rang again and one of the most enjoyable and rewarding periods of my working life was about to start.

But before I rekindle those memories, let me take you back to the very beginning: the time of my ancestors, and the upbringing that sent me out into a world that was beyond the imagination of my childhood.

Nick Hampton

Nick Hampton meeting Diana Ross

Richard Simmons receives a gold record from Nick Hampton

Nick Hampton and Clive Robbins

Col Joye and Nick Hampton with a doctor at Westmead Hospital

*Jean Panther and Nick Hampton at the
White House reception for CISAC delegates*

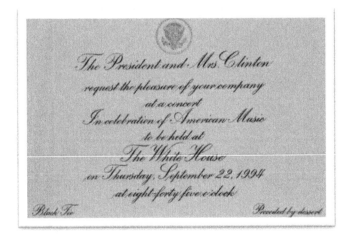

The President and Mrs. Clinton
request the pleasure of your company
at a concert
In celebration of American Music
to be held at
The White House
on Thursday, September 22, 1994
at eight-forty-five o'clock

Black Tie   Preceded by dessert

White House invitation

PROGRAM

Patti Austin	MEDLEY:	
	The Blues Is An Old Old Story	Alan Bergman Marilyn Bergman Paul Weston
	Amazing Grace	Traditional
	MEDLEY: The Blues Is A Trav'lin Thing	Alan Bergman Marilyn Bergman Paul Weston
	Blues In The Night	Harold Arlen Johnny Mercer
Ruth Brown	Nobody Knows You When You're Down and Out	Jimmie Cox
	If I Can't Sell It, I'll Keep Sittin' On It	Alexander Hill Andy Razaf
Booker T & the MG's Steve Cropper Donald "Duck" Dunn Booker T. Jones Steve Potts	Green Onions	Steve Cropper Al Jackson, Jr. Booker T. Jones Lewis Steinberg
	Time Is Tight	Steve Cropper Donald "Duck" Dunn Al Jackson, Jr. Booker T. Jones
Ashford and Simpson	MEDLEY: Ain't Nothin' Like The Real Thing You're All I Need Ain't No Mountain High Enough Reach Out And Touch	All songs by Nickolas Ashford and Valerie Simpson
Jon Hendricks	Royal Garden Blues	Clarence Williams Spencer Williams
	(Everyday) I Have The Blues	Peter Chatman
The Pointer Sisters Anita Pointer June Pointer Ruth Pointer	I'm So Excited	Anita Pointer June Pointer Ruth Pointer
	Chain Of Fools	Don Covay
Lyle Lovett	That's Right, You're Not From Texas	All songs by Lyle Lovett
	Penguins	
Michael Bolton	Georgia On My Mind	Hoagy Carmichael Stuart Gorrell
	(Sitting On The) Dock of the Bay	Steve Cropper Otis Redding
Finale	Well Alright Okay You Win	Mayne Watts Sidney Wyche

White House program of artists

129

*Jimmy Barnes and Iva Davies performing
at the Art of Music auction*

Jimmy Barnes and Ben Quilty at the Art of Music

*Nick Hampton and Jean Panther with Alex Jeliba
at the 1984 APRA Awards*

Ken East and Nick Hampton meet Itzhak Perlman

Nick Hampton welcomes the NSW Governor, Dame Marie Bashir, to the Nordoff-Robbins Music Therapy Centre

The centre's official opening: Nick Hampton standing next to Dame Marie Bashir

SECTION THREE:
LET'S GET BACK
TO THE START

17. Ground Floor . . . Going Up

NATURE or nurture? Genes or environment? Must it not be all of these, combined with timing, geography and luck, which go to making up a person and a life?

Born in 1937, I was a "pre-war baby". Ten years later and I would have been a "baby boomer". Did World War II affect my life? Of course it did.

From the age of four I was effectively the only child of a single parent and then, at nine, I regained a father whom I only vaguely knew, and who not unreasonably wanted to share my mother.

On my tenth birthday I started at a new school in a new town while my mother and father struggled to save the tailoring business they had taken over from my grandfather. Life in 1947 was not that great, and in some respects almost worse than during the war. Just about everything was still rationed and most people felt a bit let-down. During the war they knew they had to make sacrifices but now, two years later, living conditions were hardly any better and they stayed that way for several more years.

In 1950, I went to Eastbourne College and had the privilege of "fagging", which meant being one of the younger boys on call to do menial tasks – like cleaning rugger boots and blancoing cricket pads – for the prefects and seniors, as well as being beaten by prefects for minor offences like being late for . . . well just about anything. All character-building stuff of course.

This has to be put into the perspective of time and place, and one of the mainstays of those years was England's class system. The Hampton family was lower middle class. They were in "trade", and I suffered a few insults at Eastbourne on that score. Most of my contemporaries were the sons of army officers, clergymen, school teachers and small-time professionals, those who considered themselves as "middle middle class" or even "upper middle class".

In 1966, John Cleese, all six foot four, did a marvellous sketch on TV with Ronnie Barker, around five-ten, and Ronnie Corbett, who nudged five foot two, where they were dressed respectively in a bowler hat, a trilby and a cloth cap. Cleese, looking at Barker, said, "I look down on him" and then Barker (looking at Cleese) said, "I look up to him" and (turning to Corbett) "but down on him." And so it went, lampooning the snobbish differences between "dinner", "supper" and "tea" and other class usage. Today, few men wear a hat and the class system seems to have been replaced by the rich and the rest.

Yet the Hampton family had serious ambitions to be what was later called upwardly mobile; in those days it was just a question of "getting on". So in 1954, I took my Father's advice and an opportunity he created and started five years of Articles – like being indentured or apprenticed – to become a Chartered Accountant. Yes, I know, the most boring profession in the world, but one that opened up the world to me.

This memoir is not a warts-and-all dissection of my personal life. I know the mistakes I've made and the unhappiness I have caused. I set out attempting to put the events of my life – particularly my working life – in some sort of historical context. And now I hope you'll find some of the next bit, about my upbringing, entertaining.

*   *   *

1937 is not a year that really stands out in the history books. Stanley Baldwin resigned as Britain's Prime Minister and was succeeded by Neville Chamberlain, who gained everlasting infamy the following year when he returned from Munich with his "peace in our time" declaration to appease Hitler. On the twenty-sixth of April, 1937, the dictator General Franco, with German assistance, bombed the town of Guernica during the Spanish Civil War and gave Europe an ominous taste of what lay ahead.

Enough of the historical background. What about me?

I was born just before midnight on the sixteenth of February in New Malden, not far from Kingston-on-Thames. Just to the south-west of London, it was mostly built in the 1930s and my parents had bought 10 Beechcroft Avenue in 1932.

This area was a housing development for a lower middle class of tradesmen, clerical workers and junior professionals. Each red-roofed, three-bedroom "semi" cost £950, which was quite a lot if you consider that my father was earning only £10 per week, and these houses were mostly financed through the relatively new institution of a building society. New Malden was a typical dormitory suburb with a fifteen-minute walk – or a short bus ride on the 213 – to Norbiton station, from which you could catch a train to Waterloo or, changing trains at Clapham Junction, to Victoria where my father worked. It was designed with some variety in its tree-lined avenues, crescents and drives, and even had tennis courts and a community centre.

I can only imagine that for the first two and a half years I was doted on and overfed. Earliest photos show me as well-rounded and bald-headed, earning me the nickname of "Musso" after the Italian dictator.

But come the autumn of 1939, everything changed.

*   *   *

Childhood memories are supposed to be full of things like running through sunlit fields and being greeted by a mother and father picknicking by a gently flowing stream.

Sorry, I don't have that childhood.

World War II began on the third of September, 1939, and a year later the Germans started the day and night bombing offensive which became known as The Blitz. Many houses in and around London had an Anderson shelter (named after the Home Secretary of the day) supplied by the government. It was supposed to save us from anything other than a direct hit, but being built of unlined brick in our garage it was either hot and dusty or cold and dusty. After one bad air raid when my asthma started Mother said she would rather die indoors than stay another night in the shelter, and for a time, when the bombs seemed to be falling particularly close by, we would huddle in the cupboard under the stairs (where it was always hot and dusty).

Each pair of semi-detached houses shared a shelter, so we saw a lot of our neighbours Vi and George Elliott. Vi (Aunty Wye) was the first love of my life but I was frightened of George. While I knew they had terrible rows – you could hear them through the wall – it didn't occur to me that he beat her up. Father and Mother knew of course and gave their support to Vi, which increased the tension whenever George appeared. It was another early memory: I could detect the smell of fear. George, like many bullies, was afraid.

In 1940, I caught whooping cough which, combined with the asthma, came close to stopping my breathing altogether. In those days the conventional wisdom for the relief of asthma, as prescribed by the rotund but delightful Dr Kelly, was to use kaolin poultices. Kaolin is a clay used in fine china and employed hot. So it was for me: the kaolin was heated as high as deemed bearable (I once insisted that Mother tried it first and it took the skin off the end of her nose), spread onto cloths, slapped onto my chest and back, and bandaged tight. When it finally cooled and set – like plaster of paris – it would be peeled off like a giant band-aid. The fact that the "cure" was far more terrifying than the problem – and had little positive effect – went unrecognised for many months.

In 1941, the government provided us with a different type of shelter, a Morrison shelter (named after the new Home Secretary). These ones were for indoor use, self-constructed like a big Meccano set and also supposed to save us from anything except a direct hit. I remember the night Father, who was a part-time air-raid warden, heard the siren, sat up, hit his forehead on the steel rim and knocked himself out. When he came to and went on duty his officer asked him where the bomb had landed!

But now I'm going to look for that gently flowing stream . . .

18. Keylocks and Hamptons

THE Keylock family came from the village of Latton in Wiltshire and set themselves up as builders' merchants in Deptford, south-east London, at some time in the late 19th century. By the early 1900s they had also become developers in the expanding London property market, buying land on ninety-nine-year leases to build and rent houses.

James Keylock was born in 1867, so he was in his forties when he decided that he had sufficient rental income to leave London and become a gentleman farmer in Sussex. Unfortunately, James quickly discovered he was neither a gentleman nor a farmer, but he was a good builder and his first project was to build a house in Hooe for his wife Minnie and their family as well as stables and barns for his herd of dairy cows. The house looked westwards towards the Pevensey marshes and Eastbourne. In 1912, this would have been a long way even from Bexhill, and I remember Aunty Ann, my mother's older sister, telling me of being taken by pony and trap to the hospital in Hastings – nearly twenty miles away – when she had appendicitis. That must have been a frightening journey along the dirt roads.

The Keylocks did not stay long in Hooe, and over the next twenty years James built houses in Winchelsea, Rye, and at least three in Bexhill, the last being Beachend in Richmond Grove. Up until the 1960s this had an uninterrupted view of the western end of the Bexhill promenade.

I imagine that the family led a very quiet life, as James did not make friends or encourage his children to bring theirs home. He spoke rarely and I recall being at the lunch table when I was about nine and all three daughters and their husbands were present, but there was no conversation. He had, however, an affinity with small children and he would take me to his greenhouse and put me up on the potting bench while he tended his plants. No talking though.

During the war all the beaches on the south coast of England were protected against the expected German invasion by barbed wire, and there were concrete blocks and anti-tank barricades in all streets leading inland. Beachend was actually between a barricade and the beach, and Grandpa cut a secret door in his back fence and once took me for a walk along the deserted promenade. Mother was furious. I was thrilled.

Granny Keylock was totally subservient to James. She kept house, cooked, and had all her supplies delivered. If she went out it was but rarely. But she was always pleased to see her daughters and grandchildren, and I have happy memories of the breaks we'd take in Bexhill when my Mother couldn't stand life virtually on her own during the years 1941-46 when my Father was in the Army.

Doris, my Mum, who always got Dorrie, was born in 1908 in Deptford. She had three sisters, Ann, Caroline and Mary, and a brother James, but Caroline and James died very young.

Dorrie and her sisters didn't get a proper education. She left school when she was fourteen and Grandpa didn't believe his girls should work, so they stayed at home in Bexhill and helped their mother until they got married. This attitude had a profound effect on Dorrie.

Ann married Thomas Grey and their son Stanley was born in 1924. Mary married Herbert (Bert) Gill and had a daughter, Sally, in 1938, and a son, James, in 1946. In about 1948 the family emigrated as "ten pound Poms" to Australia, where Sally and Jim lived until their recent deaths and where Sally's children still live. Grandpa died in 1946 after several years of heart problems, but Minnie lived in Bexhill until she was well over ninety.

*   *   *

If Grandpa Keylock was reclusive and unwelcoming of strangers, Grandpa Hampton and his family were the opposite.

Robert Charles Hampton came from Gloucestershire and his wife Gertrude Fanny from Worcestershire, and they were into everything in Bexhill from their arrival in 1908 until well after World War II.

Robert, a tall man who became quite corpulent, was always talking and laughing, and his children took after him. Gertrude was tiny, less than five foot tall in her children's shoes. Dark and gypsy-like, with multiple rings on all her fingers, she was a marvellous hostess and matriarch, always making sure her grandchildren got the silver threepenny pieces in their slices of pudding.

Robert and Gertrude had four children: Robert (nicknamed Rowie), Ivor Gordon, my Father, also known as Dick (Doughie), Katherine *aka* Larry (Tutters) and John (Apple). People must have thought it was a family of ten! Always close and protective of each other, they even developed a secret language which they were able to speak well into middle age.

My Dad was born on the fifteenth of March, 1906, in Bedfordshire, and the family moved to Bexhill-on-Sea in 1908 when grandfather took over a tailoring business from a Mr Maconie. The boys went to a private boarding school near Eastbourne, and afterwards Robert was articled, which cost quite a lot of money in those days, to a chartered accountant (this had a big bearing on my own career choice). Dick was apprenticed to become a tailor and John joined the men's outfitting trade in a shop in High Wycombe.

The Hamptons lived over the shop in St Leonards Road in a flat which had a big living room, a dining room, kitchen and three bedrooms. There were workrooms above for the tailoring staff which were reached by an external staircase. I doubt that would pass today's OH&S standards. In the living room was a massive palm tree and a much-used piano which all four children could and did play, without waiting for an invitation.

Grandpa Hampton – who was the co-founder of the Bexhill Building Society and Rotary, and also became Deputy Mayor on the town council and Deputy Grand Master of the Masonic Lodge – taught me how to play cribbage, solo, whist and rummy before

I was six. I think that's how I learned to count. All the Hamptons were great games players, and during their teens and early twenties the children were a force in the social and sporting life of Bexhill, helping to set up a tennis and a hockey club. Which is how Dick met Dorrie.

All the children married and all three boys went to the war.

Robert married Phyllis and they had twins, Richard and Rosalie. Robert joined the Royal Army Pay Corps, became a Major, and was "mentioned in dispatches" in the landing at Anzio. By his account this was because he continued to play a bridge match with his CO while under heavy fire.

Dick joined the Royal Army Ordnance Corps in 1941, was commissioned, and gained the rank of Captain. By September '44, the German army had been pushed out of northern France and he was posted to Roubaix to run a large textiles plant and distribution centre, where he remained until April 1946.

Kathleen married Harry and they had three children: Pat, Jill and Penny. Harry served in an anti-aircraft battery and was killed in the war and Kathleen remarried to Harold, a retired professional soldier.

John married Brenda and they had three children: Anne, Christopher and Sandra. He served in the artillery in the North African and Italian campaigns.

Of the grandchildren, all but Pat and Christopher survive.

*   *   *

Dick and Dorrie's personalities reflected those of their families: he was outgoing, gregarious and always ready for games while she was almost painfully shy and retiring. But perhaps it was the differences that brought them together, and they were married in 1932.

They moved into a flat in Queen's Road, Wimbledon, before buying the house in New Malden. Dick had already become a "Military Cutter", which meant he specialised in cutting uniforms for officers in the armed forces, as well as dignitaries. One of his clients was Joachim von Ribbentrop, Germany's Ambassador to

England, who used a tailoring firm called H. Plumb & Co. in Victoria Street. Von Ribbentrop was notorious for keeping his tailors waiting for hours and gained a reputation in British high society for being pompous and conceited. On returning to Germany in 1938 he was appointed by Hitler as Foreign Minister, and in 1946 he was the first of the high-ranking Nazis to be hanged after the Nuremberg war crimes trials.

Dorrie stayed home, so everything was set for a mostly happy marriage which lasted until 1975.

19. Wartime

BECAUSE we lived on the outskirts of London we endured The Blitz in 1940-41 and then the "flying bombs" (V-1 and V-2) in 1944-45. Father was away in the Army and rarely got home leave, so it was hardly surprising that Mother got lonely and probably depressed. She had to put up with me too.

Quite often we would go off by train to stay with distant relatives, occasionally in Bexhill, but it copped a lot of bombing too, so more frequently we'd go to Dick's aunts in Worcester or Dorrie's in Amersham, where we stayed with Uncle Maurice and Aunty Ada.

I loved it there and I think Maurice and Ada did too. They had no children because Ada had a spinal disorder. She wore a caliper and had to be carried upstairs by Maurice. Nevertheless, or perhaps because of it, they were devoted to each other and to the Methodist church where Maurice was a lay preacher.

They had a small house on Amersham Common, no bathroom and an outside loo. But to me it was heaven. Uncle Maurice put up a swing and built a pond with a windmill in the middle. He was a foreman roadworker and rode off each day on his motorcycle, which had a sidecar for Ada when they went to church or the shops. If it was cold or wet he would put layers of newspaper between his leather coat and his suit, which he always wore with a stiff-collared shirt and a tie. Friday evening was bath night and Mother and Aunty Ada boiled kettles to half-fill a large metal tub. I was first in and then it was Uncle Maurice's turn.

Dorrie and I went on long walks. My favourite was to Chesham Bois, along the way picking up watercress from the stream at the side of the road and, oh joy of joys, if the old lady in the cottage at Chesham was cooking, jam-filled doughnuts. You could smell them from afar and she sold them for two a penny. Those outings made me fascinated by the memorial to the poor martyrs from the Middle Ages who were put into barrels which were set alight and rolled down Amersham Hill.

In Old Amersham, Auntie Emily and Uncle Will lived in a little "Dick Turpin" cottage, so-called because the legendary highwayman was supposed to have stayed there. It was minute, one up and one down with a loo at the bottom of the garden. Presumably Uncle Will used the "daily deposits" to fertilise the veggies or threw them into the canal. He would always greet me by saying "'Ello tuppence, or is it sixpence?" and slip a small coin into my hand.

At least two of Dorrie's other aunts lived in Amersham, so for me it was always like going back to a very warm and safe place. Except for one Sunday when I was in bed (yes, with asthma), everyone else was at church, and a V-2 fell on a house less than a hundred yards away. A very big bang, a long pause . . . and then the sound of Dorrie running along the street. It was a near miss.

*   *   *

At home in Beechcroft Avenue I don't think I was any different to most little boys: my first railway set was clockwork, probably the best thing I have ever owned in my life. It was permanently set up in the dining room and steadily added to with cars and trucks, soldiers (made of lead, which must have been another health hazard) and a wonderful wooden farm with buildings and animals. The farm was hand-made by my Mother, who inherited so many of the practical skills of her Father.

As a small boy, I played games with Mother and I remember having a cricket bat quite early on. She also used to take me for cycle rides, with me perched on the carrier. Our favourite was up Coombe Hill and into Richmond Park, which had a big army training camp. The soldiers used to wolf-whistle at Mother, and I was rather proud.

She built me a sandpit as well as a tree-house, and I spent a lot of time in them while Mother looked after the vegetable garden. There were peas, beans, radishes and lettuces, and mustard and cress grown on wet paper in boxes. Plus fruit: her raspberries and gooseberries were fantastic, and what we didn't eat immediately was stored in Kilner jars.

We listened to the radio a lot, *Children's Hour* with Uncle Mac most afternoons and *Workers' Playtime* with Wilfred Pickles. Later on ITMA, *It's That Man Again*, a radio classic with Tommy Handley and his regulars: Mona Lott ("Can I do you now, sir?" and "It's being so cheerful what keeps me going") and the German spy ("This is Funf speaking"). The radio kept us in touch with the world.

*   *   *

From six to ten I went to a private school in New Malden called Bretby House. It was owned by a single lady, Mrs Lees, who was also the head teacher. There were only three classrooms but we managed to get a grounding in all the usual stuff and even learn a bit of Latin and French. Bretby educated youngsters with a view to getting them to a grammar school via the Eleven Plus exam, which was introduced by the government in 1944.

Of my early childhood, apart from learning my first naughty words, as in "I chased a bug around a tree" (say it quickly), I only recall playtimes in the garden and singing, accompanied by a piano driven by music rolls which were very popular in those days and are quite valuable now. Some of the songs would be considered extremely offensive these days, such as *Pollywolly Doodle*: "And I came to a river and I couldn't get across, so I jumped on a nigger 'cos I thought he was a hoss". But in those innocent days, no problems.

I would say that I was a well-behaved child, but I did occasionally let loose. My cousin Stanley gave me a clockwork mouse which I wound up and set off across the floor towards Mrs Lees, who screamed, leaped onto her chair, and had a nose bleed. I don't think I claimed ownership of the mouse.

The war was never far from us and one morning, the thirteenth of June, 1944, while Mother was walking me to school, everywhere seemed unusually quiet and deserted. We got to

Bretby House and the door was closed. We knocked. Eventually Mrs Lees arrived and said: "Didn't you hear the sirens? Come in quickly." She told us that the air-raid warnings had gone off at about six-thirty and the "All Clear" had not yet sounded. As we set off home we saw our first flying-bomb (or "doodle-bug" as they became known). It was quite small with stumpy wings and flew so low that you could see there was no pilot. Over the next year we saw and heard a lot of V-1s although none crashed and exploded near us. It was generally reckoned that if, after the motor stopped, you could count to five you were going to be okay. The V-2s, launched in September that year, were the first inter-continental rockets and much nastier – you couldn't hear them coming.

June the thirteenth was one week after D-Day, the Allied invasion of France. Reports at first were scarce though positive, whatever was happening, but as the Allied troops started gaining ground the newspapers were given enough information to print maps of their advances, and both at home and at school these were cut out and pinned on the walls. The maps and the nightly BBC news broadcasts were unmissable throughout the last year of the war which was ingrained into our everyday lives: the ration cards; the queues for everything; bolting into shelters at the wail of a siren. For small children it was something we grew up with. For our parents, mostly the mothers, it must have been immensely hard.

The war in Europe ended on the seventh of May, 1945. VE-Day was celebrated on the eighth throughout Great Britain, including Beechcroft Avenue, with bonfires and street parties, although I doubt there was much alcohol available. The following weekend a children's party was organised at the community centre where we had various races and I came last in the eight-to-tens egg-and-spoon race. Never was very competitive at sports.

And then we waited for our fathers to come home.

20. Sunny Days in Bexhill

IN the first part of the twentieth century English people were not generally used to moving around as much as they are now. The fact that both Uncle Robert and my Father had taken the step of moving to London to live and work was looked upon as quite adventurous. And except for unforeseen circumstances I would probably have spent the whole of my childhood living in New Malden.

In 1947, I was about to take the 11+ exam with the ambition of going to Kingston-on-Thames Grammar School. But in February, a week before my tenth birthday, we moved to Bexhill. I'm not sure quite why Dick and Dorrie decided to do that, and I believe there were times when they regretted it, but I think they did the right thing. It was a decision that certainly changed our lives.

The given reason was that Grandpa Hampton's tailoring business was failing and Dick had to take it over and rescue it. Which he did eventually, but it was very hard for a year or two as Grandpa had squandered – or failed to demand – clothing coupons from his wartime customers. Come 1947, he had no stock, no coupons to buy any, and the outlook was bleak: clothing would be rationed for three more years. Only a massive rally-round by the family saved the day and got the business restarted. So we took the top flat of 19 Woodville Road and rented the bottom to Uncle John and Auntie Brenda and my six-year-old cousin Ann.

Despite still suffering from the war in other ways, like the rest of Great Britain, Bexhill was beginning to recover as a holiday destination, with its three major hotels as well as dozens of "private" hotels and boarding houses. By the mid-fifties, people were also discovering it as a place to retire and Bexhill became known as the capital of the "costa geriatrica", creating more prosperity. In the next ten years its population nearly doubled as low-cost housing developments sprang up, further boosting local businesses.

The Bexhill I remember was a pleasant area to grow up in, with good sporting facilities, a nice if pebbly beach and plenty of places like Hastings, Battle and Eastbourne within a bus or short train ride. It was a safe community, and everybody knew and kept an eye out for everyone else.

Woodville Road backed onto Egerton Park, which had tennis courts and bowling greens. Children could hire a paddle boat, sail their toy boats on the pond, and enjoy the playground. On Sundays in summer the Bexhill Town Band gave concerts on the bandstand. I soon learned how to climb over the fence at the bottom of our garden and get into the park without being spotted.

*   *   *

The first pet of which I was at least a part-owner was Ginger, a magnificent tomcat with colouring like dark marmalade. I think my cousin Ann introduced him to our households, and he stayed around long after she and her family had left.

Ginger was seriously big and very agile. He could scale the six foot-high fence at the bottom of the garden with ease, although he sometimes had difficulty getting back and needed rescuing – possibly because he was gorging himself on the ducklings near the lake. Quite how Dorrie achieved a stay of execution I have no idea, but come one summer the head park keeper ensured that all ducklings were born on the island in the middle of the lake, where they belonged. Ginger was a real character. He walked around with a proprietorial air being petted by all the old ladies. When he died at the amazing age of twenty-two the local newspaper, the *Bexhill Observer*, gave him an obituary including a photograph.

I also kept white mice in beautiful cages with wheels and ladders and runways and nesting boxes, all crafted by my talented Mother. We used to make racetracks for them in the garden and it was generally believed that they ran faster if they had a dab of butter on their noses. (Some children will believe anything!)

I also had a three-legged tortoise called George.

*   *   *

For me, the biggest change in 1947 was going to a new school. Bretby House was run by middle-aged women who were kind and gentle with the sixty or so young girls and boys in their charge. I was completely unprepared for Harewood Preparatory School in Bexhill, and I doubt that my parents had done any research.

Harewood was a boys-only school teaching enough to get its charges aged up to thirteen through the Common Entrance exam and into the Public School chosen by the parents. That was its role in theory. In practice, remembering that the war had ended only eighteen months earlier, it was taking any boy whose parents could pay. At one end of the age scale we had three brothers (the Browns major, minor and minimus), the youngest of whom was no more than five and had to be carried by a prefect when we went on school walks. At the other end were Walker and Seary who shaved every day and caused Harewood to be banned from inter-school cricket matches because they were clearly over the age of fourteen. At the 1947 sports day, Walker threw the cricket ball clean over the cricket pavilion, it couldn't be found, and we didn't have another one, so he got the prize. How bizarre.

About half the boys were boarders, and to start with my parents arranged for me to have lunch and "tea" at school. The food was terrible: the meat was so bad we would push lumps of gristle through knot-holes in the floorboards and you could hear the rats fighting over it.

The principal and owner of Harewood was a Mr Spooner, who was not a kindly man either to his staff or pupils and had a nasty black and white dog that nipped your ankles if it spotted you feeding the rats.

The staff included Miss Ailsa Craig (surely one of the few women ever to be named after an uninhabited rock off the coast of Scotland) who taught French, Mr Hodder who taught maths and geography, and Mr Mulvaney who taught everything else . . . with some difficulty. We soon twigged that he had the lid of his

149

desk propped open so he could read the textbooks just ahead of us. And then there was the matron, Mrs Simpson, rather gorgeous, no husband, with a son aged seven. Mr Mulvaney was clearly in love with her from the moment she arrived.

The winter of '47 remains one of the coldest on record and with fuel, mostly coal in those days, still on ration, everywhere was freezing most of the time. The school's flint-hard playing field was too dangerous for sport until mid-April. That first term at Harewood stays in my memory for the awful food and the interminable walks we had every afternoon.

In 1948, Mr Spooner sold Harewood to a Reverend Woodruffe who was a better teacher and manager. We lost the over-fourteen pupils and were readmitted to the inter-school cricket and football tournaments. I even played for the first cricket eleven in the summer of 1950 – my sole representative sporting achievement.

Reverend Woodruffe did his best to please the parents by demonstrating that almost every boy had a gift which deserved recognition, and at the 1950 Sport and Speech Day I was awarded a prize. The guest of honour was the Duke of Devonshire, who announced: "The next prize is the Reliability Cup which goes to Nicholas Hampton." My parents looked so proud as I stood up and walked to the rostrum. The Duke picked up a battered cup balanced precariously on a wooden plinth and held it out to me while extending his right hand to shake mine. "Well done," he said as my fingers closed around it. For an instant I held the cup as I shook the Duke's hand, looking him in the eye while saying "Thank you, sir." And then . . . it slipped off the plinth and fell to the grass. "Not quite so reliable today, then," said His Grace. I could feel my parents dying of embarrassment.

Reverend Woodruffe certainly made great improvements to academic and sporting standards, but unfortunately he liked small boys too much and the school closed in about 1952.

*   *   *

As we were only a five-minute walk from the beach, Dick and John bought a beach cabin, so the July and August summer holidays were spent there, swimming, catching and cooking shrimp, and playing cricket on the low-tide sands. After the awful winter, the summer of 1947, our first in Bexhill, is still one of the hottest on record. All my cousins and Ann's cousins came to stay and we had one big family party from morning till evening, when Dick and John would join us for a final swim after closing up the shop. I couldn't have thought of anything better.

We didn't have iPads, computers, electronic games, DVDs, even television, let alone parents who took us everywhere by car. What we did have was freedom to roam around. Even in New Malden, by the age of six I was going off on my own to the shops; I usually went to and from school unaccompanied; and I had a bicycle. By the time I was twelve my friends and I would cycle off to the woods, five or six miles away, and spend a whole afternoon without our parents worrying if we were alright.

In the summer I could go to the beach or the swimming pool and meet up with friends and be away from home for hours, but there was always an agreed time to get back – and woe betide me if I was late! Parental concern seemed to be subordinated to the notion that we had to be allowed to make our own mistakes and learn how to take care of ourselves.

We didn't miss the lack of material possessions either, although some were prized: my first Waterman's fountain pen for instance.

21. Big School

EASTBOURNE College dates from 1867 when there was a huge upsurge in private and public education. It has never been a "top" school and few of its pupils have gone on to become famous.

When I was there the only old boys to achieve fame were two politicians: Gwilym Lloyd George (later Lord Tenby) who had various government roles culminating in Home Secretary under prime ministers Winston Churchill and Anthony Eden; and Woodrow Wyatt, a Labour Party member of parliament, for which sin he was virtually banned from college functions, but who in his later years became a journalist and admirer of Margaret Thatcher. Quite a change of thinking in his case. In my time I think only John Wells became a celebrity (more of him later), while Eddie Izzard, one of England's most celebrated comedians, was there with my son Jerry. So the score seems to be two comedians and two politicians.

In 1954, there were about five hundred pupils, all boys, of whom four hundred were boarders spread over five houses and one hundred were day boys split between two houses, Powell (pronounced "Pole") and Reeves. Our housemaster was T.D. (Teddy) Craig who lived in an upstairs flat with his wife and four children.

The scholastic program was spread over four or five years depending on how well you had done in Common Entrance. I went straight into Year 2, but was disadvantaged because I never did science. When it came time to specialise for A-Level purposes I couldn't elect to do chemistry/biology or maths, which was usually paired up with physics. So, going into the Fifth Form in 1952, I chose French and German, which I was probably best at anyway. I was lucky that our senior modern language teacher was P. W. M. Halliday, who worked on the basis that if he scared you enough to start with you wouldn't give him trouble later. He lived in another flat in Powell House with his butler/valet. Those were the days . . .

Sport, the Combined Cadet Force and chapel played a big part in school life. Five afternoons of sport a week turned me into a confirmed spectator; the Royal Air Force section of the CCF gave me a love of flying; and chapel every school morning and Evensong on Sundays gave me the grounding for becoming an atheist. In fairness, I did enjoy tennis and squash, which I continued to play for several years after leaving Eastbourne, but personal competitive exercise has always left me cold. Jerry once said publicly – at his wedding – that the only time he ever saw me run was the Open Day when he was at Eastbourne and I spotted the Bursar approaching, chasing me for unpaid fees.

The school motto was *Ex Oriente Salus*, "Salvation from the East", but it should have been "The School before the House before the Boy", and this was rammed into us from day one when all the new boys were gathered in the main hall known as Big School. Amongst others, the commanding officer of the Combined Cadet Force (nicknamed "The Barrel", no prizes for guessing why) addressed us: "I want you to all understand that there is nothing compulsory about joining the CCF, it's absolutely voluntary, and in fact only last year one boy chose not to join." We looked at each other and wondered what had happened to him and then our hands shot up to join.

However, I must admit to enjoying the year I spent in the infantry corps when we would regularly march into town singing:

> *Heidi, heidi, Christ almighty, who the hell are we.*
> *We're bugger Barrel's army and the college infantry.*

But I really loved the three years I spent in the RAF section under the charismatic leadership of a World War Two fighter ace, the very good-looking Squadron Leader Donald Perrens, who took us to camps at Cranwell (the officer training college) and the Fleet Air Arm station in Gosport, where we were allowed to take the controls of two-seater planes.

The reputation of the school was paramount and little was done to encourage individuality in the pupils – unless it was in a solo sport such as tennis, and even that was regarded with some suspicion by the "rugger buggers". Similarly, academic abilities were not highly regarded and the prefects tended to be drawn from the sporting teams. There was a strong inbuilt feeling of anti-intellectualism.

One of my friends did become famous: John Wells. An actor and writer, he was one of the early contributors to the satirical magazine *Private Eye*, for which he co-wrote Mrs Wilson's Diary and the Dear Bill letters. At Eastbourne, John excelled in languages but was not suited to sport or what was known as PE (physical education), which took place every morning under the eye of the gym master, Regimental Sergeant Major Strong. When we were doing press-ups, RSM Strong would bawl out "Down with a bounce and a bounce come up again". And against that we – and the RSM – would hear John's fluting voice: "Down with a flounce and a pout come up again." John and the RSM did not get on all that well, and sadly John died in 1998. I've kept in touch with two contemporaries, John Raeburn and Nigel Mundy, and happily they are still alive and well. I'll come back to life in Australia later, but I'll just add here that the Old Eastbournian Association flourishes "Down Under" with branches in Sydney, Melbourne and Perth. I was the organiser of the annual dinner in Sydney for several years and about twenty OEs attended. It was good to keep in touch although most of the others were younger than me, and I have to admit that hearing the same stories about life at the college year after year was beginning to wear a bit thin.

I took French and German as my "A" level subjects in 1954 and passed both. My other achievement in that final year was winning the C.W. Mackenzie Senior German Prize, and I'm sure my parents were very proud when I was presented with it on Speech Day and didn't drop it.

Current affairs were never on the curriculum and there was little discussion of domestic politics. It was assumed that everyone at a Public School would be a Conservative Party supporter, as the Labour Party was full of dangerous lunatics intent on destroying the country.

But we were aware of world events outside Britain. In June 1950, just before I started at Eastbourne, North Korea invaded the South and what we feared would become a third World War erupted. Many lives were lost when the United Kingdom joined the conflict, including the older brother of one of my school friends.

After being dumped by voters in 1945, Churchill, who was still revered for his wartime leadership, defeated Clem Atlee at the 1951 general election and ruled for another four years. The British Bulldog, with his Chancellor R.A. Butler, rekindled the economic recovery of the fifties as the nation emerged from the long years of gloom.

*   *   *

We started to take holidays in France, and my first experience was a school trip from Harewood to Dinard at Easter in 1950. A party of eight, including Miss Craig and two older boys, set off from Portsmouth on the overnight ferry to Jersey. Then we *flew* to St Malo in a Douglas DC-3 carrying twenty-five passengers after taking off from a reasonably flat field. At the age of thirteen we thought we were in heaven.

In 1951, Dick managed to get sufficient currency together (there were still exchange controls in operation) and hire a car, and off the three of us went to France. First to Roubaix by the Belgian border, seeing where he had been posted back in '44. That evening he took us to a bar and a charming waitress came up and said, "*Bonsoir*, Captain Hampton, it is a pleasure to see you again!" I had the feeling that Mother was not happy.

From there we drove through the First World War battlefields in northern France and into Paris, still dirty and unkempt but the Paris my father loved nonetheless. We stayed with the Johnsons, who opened up their house in the suburb of Garches to British Army officers when they returned to it in late 1944. They came to Paris to live in 1912 and, having survived the Great War without leaving the city, assumed they could do the same in May 1940. They got out just before the Germans reached Paris and escaped to England by boat from Bordeaux. Mr Johnson was bilingual, with upper-echelon French connections including General de Gaulle. He proved very useful to the Allies and served in Roubaix as a liaison officer alongside my father.

Mrs Johnson was *formidable*, to use the French word. Armed with her white bull terrier and a walking stick to hit it on the nose, she terrorised the shopkeepers of Garches. Actually Jemima, the dog, just wanted to be loved, which I discovered, and we became friends. She would come with me, straining at her leash and me whacking her on the nose, when I went to the village dairy where the milk came directly from the cows at the back of the shop via huge pails into my two-litre milk can.

For several years I was invited by the Johnsons to spend Easter with them, which started my own love affair with Paris. After my first visit and a lot of walking around the city with Mrs J she was happy for me to go off on my own. Today, can you imagine a fourteen-year-old boy being put on a train by his mother, expected to change onto a cross-channel ferry, and then take another train to be met in Paris? Pretty much left to his own devices? I don't think so.

*   *   *

I was "put down" for Keble College, Oxford, to read modern languages, but in 1954 National Service was still compulsory and Oxford was only taking new students either post-service or over the age of nineteen. As I wasn't fit enough for National Service and had to wait two years before going to Oxford, my Father played a clever card. He had always wanted me to be a chartered accountant and now he said: "If you do two years of Articles with a firm of CAs you could still go to Oxford in a couple of years' time." (I used that little trick in 1978 when Juliet wanted to go to the Royal Academy of Dramatic Art and become an actress. One does occasionally learn something useful from your parents.) So school was over and becoming a chartered accountant seemed to be a reasonably attractive proposition. Yes, I know that chartered accountancy *is* the most boring profession in the world, but maybe I was lucky. I had a great time with it . . . mostly.

22. Work, Work, Work

HAVING persuaded me to try accountancy, Dick did not take long to find a CA firm that would take me on as an Articled Clerk. "Articled" meant that I had to sign up for five years, during which time I would receive training and time off to study and take exams. In reality, this meant I didn't have to work on Saturday mornings. And quite surprising for that era, instead of Dick having to pay them a "premium" to employ me, they paid me £2 per week. I was the first articled clerk in Kent and Sussex to get a deal like that.

So in September 1954, at the age of seventeen years and seven months, I started work at Creasey, Son & Wickenden in Tunbridge Wells where my "principal" was Brigadier Eric Walter Peter Broad, who was also a Bexhill resident and a client of my Father.

CS&W had four partners and three offices – Tunbridge Wells, London and Bexhill – but most of the audit and tax work was centred on Tunbridge Wells and it was widespread: hotels, shops, farms, solicitors, though mostly small businesses, a lot of them providing incomplete records. You would often be presented with a box of bank statements and invoices and told to "write up the books". Sometimes this was done in the CS&W offices and sometimes at the client's and, if the latter, I would normally be accompanied by a senior clerk.

The office in Tunbridge Wells was located in Lonsdale Gardens in a three-storey Edwardian-style house comprising three large audit rooms, each with a senior clerk plus up to six juniors, and individual offices for three partners and two chief clerks. I worked there for nearly three years and gained experience in every audit room. The only one I disliked was the one run by Mr Walker, a strict "exclusive" member of the Plymouth Brethren church who allowed no talking. Either by fate or design, one of the other clerks was also in the Plymouth Brethren, a man called Penfold, one of the more "open" variety. Being from mutually excluding groups within the same religion, these two hated each other. Penfold did me a great service by introducing me to homeopathy, which played a huge part in stopping major asthma attacks.

The senior chief clerk was Charlie Wiggins. Aged in his late fifties, Charlie (always called Mr Wiggins to his face) was typical I think of that era. "Where do you go for holidays?" I once asked him. "Always go to the same place," he replied. "Nice little private boarding house on the Isle of Wight. Been going there for thirty years and know the people there pretty well. They even let us help with the washing up."

The other articled clerk in that office was Ron Sweetman, a local Tunbridge Wells lad about four years older than me. Ron was appalled by my ingrained Conservatism and soon had me reading the *New Statesman* and getting interested in jazz. The more I read the more I felt that the Tories did not represent the sort of person I wanted to be.

It was also at CS&W that I met James Evill, who became a close and longstanding friend and introduced me to scotch (I'm talking about the whisky!)

In May 1957, I passed the intermediate exam and asked if I could transfer to the London office in Chancery Lane to broaden my experience. This was agreed to when Uncle Robert (now very well known in the City of London as finance director of Cable & Wireless Holdings Limited, a unit trust and successor to the huge international communications company) intervened. He also offered me accommodation in Friern Barnet. Already "who you knew" was becoming more important than "what you knew".

The London office had all sorts of clients and I was sent on audits of companies in Portsmouth, Bournemouth and Kingston-on-Thames. Being older, I was treated more as a senior clerk and sometimes took a junior or a comptometrist with me.

One of our new clients was a small engineering business which set up an injection moulding plant near Bournemouth, Edward Webster & Co Ltd. They only had one product, but it was a beauty:

the first lipstick dispenser with a spiral mechanism. You twisted the dispenser rather than pushing it up and down and leaving lipstick smudged around the top. The two men responsible for this simple but ingenious invention were Edward Webster, a tough little Eastender, and Leonard Machin, who was previously employed by REVLON. Machin had seen the need for the lipstick dispenser, Webster knew how to make it, and REVLON had promised to buy the entire output of their factory for an agreed price, giving them a huge marketing advantage in the global cosmetics industry.

Brian Woods and I were sent in to do an audit, which meant producing accounts as no financial reporting had been provided during the year. All the proprietors knew was that they had cash in the bank – a lot.

After working on the books for a week Brian and I realised we could not explain the company's huge profit. Yet everything balanced. We called the London partner and asked him to get down to Bournemouth ASAP. He was not happy. But our accounts were accepted and correct – and we figured out the puzzle. The actual cost of manufacturing the lipstick dispensers was approximately *half* of Edward's production forecast. He was a great engineer but no accountant. The unaccounted-for sum of a million pounds in the bank was a taxable profit.

By the following year Machin had taken care of the profit problem. He bought a shell company quoted on the Birmingham Stock Exchange called Cope Allman Limited, which then bought Edward Webster & Co as well as several companies with tasty assets but business losses. Leonard Machin had invented "asset stripping".

In my last year at CS&W I was offered the job of chief accountant with Cope Allman, reporting to the now rather famous Len Machin. As the offer was made hours after the current CA was nearly killed in a road accident caused by stress I turned it down.

I had realised, however, that my goal would be to find a career in industry, and to do that I needed the experience and cachet of working for a major firm. With some more of Uncle Robert's help I got another offer, from Price Waterhouse & Co, straight after I qualified and completed my Articles in 1959. Five years had gone by and I had hardly given Oxford another thought. I was engaged to Valerie, earning £750 a year, and contemplating a mortgage!

PW&Co in those days was pretty archaic. Housed in a building in Old Jewry near the Bank of England, it had the maximum twenty partners then allowed by law, about sixty senior managers and five hundred clerks, of whom some twenty per cent were articled and the rest, like me, newly qualified. If you hadn't been offered a manager's position by the age of thirty the rule of thumb was that you should consider moving on. Controlling this vast horde of worker bees was the staff partner. In my day it was Mr Martin Harris, who also came from Bexhill. Remember, this was well before the advent of computers – most books of account and records were kept manually and on accounting machines. Let me try to paint the scene.

Every Friday morning Mr Harris would sit just inside the Partners' Room on the ground floor with a huge ledger in which our names were cross-referenced with the jobs we were working on. On entering the room, one would say, "Good morning, sir. Hampton. Shell Petroleum. Two more weeks, and I need two assistants and a comptometrist for a day." Mr Harris would consult his ledger, compare your response with the week before and allocate staff, asking questions as appropriate. He was truly amazing: once seen, he never forgot a face or a name. After this consultation you exited by another door, getting a glance at the other nineteen partners smoking and drinking coffee. This weekly ritual, of you being part of the regimentation of perhaps one hundred and fifty people marching in, through and out of the Partners' Room, was known as "Going through the book".

I was with PW&Co for almost two years, during which time I got married and acquired a baby, a house and a mortgage. Though mostly enjoyable times, some of the audits were mind-numbingly dull.

Like many of my young colleagues I read the "Situations Vacant" ads in *The Daily Telegraph* each morning and one day I saw this: "Associated Television Ltd. seeks a young, qualified Chartered Accountant for the newly created position of Assistant to the Group Accountant." My handwritten application was in that day, interviews followed and that's how I suddenly turned up at Great Cumberland Place, Marble Arch, in mid-1962 as a very junior member of the United Kingdom's first independent (meaning commercial) television company and the only company to have a seven-day broadcasting licence.

I had an office to myself on the fourth floor and a salary of £1,350 a year plus a virtually guaranteed bonus of twenty per cent – wealth beyond compare! Trouble is, I've always found that my requirements easily kept up with my means.

As we've seen, ATV was where I started on my career in the entertainment and music business which lasted forty-five years, up until 2007. A career that took me to so many fabulous places around the world and introduced me to all those people who have been . . . well, my life.

23. And Some Play

WHEN I left Eastbourne in 1954 I had few friends of my own in Bexhill, so I was happy to find that one of my neighbours was also travelling up to work in Tunbridge Wells each day. This was Norman Frake, and for a few years we were close buddies despite an age difference of about eight years.

Norman worked for Martins Bank and still lived at home with his parents, who owned a big three-storey place in Woodville Road which they kept both as a guest house and for lodgers. More importantly for me, Norman had a motorbike, a Triumph Tiger 500, which to the non-technical meant it went bloody fast. Over the next couple of years I was the fairly constant pillion rider. Locally we went to many motor car and motorcycle races, and in August 1955 we made a fifteen-day trip of over two thousand miles through France and Switzerland.

Although I'd been to France with my parents and stayed with the Johnsons this was my first "grown-up" adventure. Did my parents worry? Fortunately Norman was older, had done this sort of trip before, and seemed pretty level-headed. Besides, I was eighteen and legally an adult. But I'm sure they worried a bit, and remember there were no mobile phones back then and a postcard took about a week to cross the Channel.

My memories of our big trip are staying in a lot of hostels and small hotels and meeting plenty of other English "bikies" (although the term had not yet been invented). We followed a rough itinerary, incorporating at my insistence several legs of that year's Tour de France which included the Col du Forclaz. It turned out to be so steep that on some sections I had to dismount and walk because Norman couldn't keep the front wheel on the road. Each evening we took pot-luck and found somewhere affordable to stay. The hostel in Chamonix, looking from our room over to

Mont Blanc, the little hotel in Eze with the breathtaking view down to and over the Mediterranean, and the brothel in Nice (well we were very innocent and it looked okay from the outside, and the girls were nice, but not for us) are probably the standouts. We also stayed a couple of nights with the Johnsons and I showed Norman "my" Paris.

By the summer of 1956 I had acquired a girlfriend, Elizabeth, and when I found out that she was going to Sitges in Spain with her parents in August I talked Norman into following them in his newly acquired car, an elderly Riley with a split windscreen and running boards. I don't think Liz's parents were too happy, and Norman must have been mad to agree to such a plan, but it worked out quite well. He and I camped on Sitges beach while Liz and the parents were in a hotel. During the day the three of us explored, swam, walked and lunched together and the parents relaxed.

Sitges in 1956 was a small, undeveloped and undiscovered village with an excellent sandy beach you could drive onto. Food and wine were cheap but some of the locals weren't too friendly. One time when Liz was wearing a sun dress with bare shoulders we were surrounded by elderly women who spat at her. We went to Barcelona and saw a bullfight. It was a marvellous spectacle but, unlike Hemingway whom I'd read extensively, I wasn't overwhelmed by the bravery of the *toreros*, who seemed to have the odds heavily stacked in their favour.

The following summer my parents took Liz and me to Switzerland. The country around Interlaken and Grindelwald was magic but my relationship with Liz was not, and it finished when we got back to England.

*   *   *

Music in the 1950s was something you listened to on radio or bought on record – shellac in those days – but it was the heyday of the musical, with the great productions from America like *South Pacific*, *Oklahoma!* and *The Sound of Music* packing out London's theatres. My mother loved them and I did too after seeing my first musical, Novello's *Perchance to Dream*, at the Coliseum in 1946. I went with my parents, and Dad was still in uniform.

In the late '50s, *My Fair Lady* was a huge hit. I saw it early in its long run with Rex Harrison and Julie Andrews. But the show I most enjoyed and still remember vividly was *Salad Days* by Julian Slade and Dorothy Reynolds, which had a song I particularly liked about never looking back.

Salad Days ran for more than two thousand performances in the West End and I saw it with three different girlfriends. I married the last one (at least I wouldn't have to see the show again). It would seem terribly camp nowadays, but Slade and I were about the same age, the show seemed so romantic and innocent, and "looking forward" was what we were all doing.

*   *   *

In my teens we certainly partied, but this often took the form of going to dances. Not discos, which I am happy to recall were not invented until well into the '60s, but real dances with a band. Some were held in hotels where you could also have dinner, but we'd just go for a night of dancing, and perhaps follow up with early "breakfast" at two in the morning. Several hotels in Hastings and Eastbourne held these dances on Saturday evenings and you had to dress up to get in: dinner jackets and bow ties for the boys, at least cocktail dresses for the girls. Pretty formal, but we enjoyed it.

I had met Valerie Priest (later Rose) at a fundraising dance in Bexhill some time in 1956. Her father was the Barclays Bank manager in Lewes, where the family lived literally "over the bank". Her mother was heavily involved in fundraising for the Red Cross and did not allow the wallflowers at her dances to sit around. She paired off unattached boys and girls and made sure they enjoyed themselves, as long as that involved dancing, and not too closely. Drinking alcohol was not encouraged, although there may have been some beer for the boys and the celebrated non-alcoholic Baby Cham for the girls.

In April 1957, Valerie sent me an invitation to the twenty-first birthday party of one of her best friends, Valerie Spencer, at the Grand Hotel in Eastbourne, and for once we all put our hands in our pockets and paid for the dinner and dance. Valerie (Spencer) was wearing a long, pale-coloured dress with so many underskirts that it flared out . . . not quite enough. I managed to put my foot on the hem as we did a turn and nearly pulled it off. Not too embarrassing for her, but I was surprised that she ever spoke to me again.

At that time we both had "others", so Valerie and I didn't start going out until the following summer when her boyfriend, John Davis, went on a holiday in Europe and I promised to look after her in his absence. Let's just say I did and the relationship blossomed, which put John's nose right out of joint when he got back.

Valerie was working at Bexhill Town Hall before moving on to become secretary to the manager of Barclays Bank in St Leonards, while by this time I was in London all week and usually got back to Bexhill just for the weekend. We were engaged shortly after I passed my finals in 1959 and had a marvellous holiday that summer when we drove up to Scotland and the Mull of Kintyre, where John Rose, who had married Valerie Priest the previous year, was the engineering officer on a highly secret experimental submarine.

In September 1960, we were married at the church of St Barnabas in Bexhill and had a reception for almost one hundred at the Granville Hotel. Then we drove to London, stayed in Brown's Hotel for the night, flew to Nice and took a bus to Alassio, just over the border in Italy.

*   *   *

Although Bexhill was almost a perfect town to grow up in, Valerie and I felt hemmed in; we knew there was something more "out there". Whilst having the two incomes would enable us to save, the daily train journey to and from London was wearing, particularly if I was auditing outside Central London, and I had a minimum twelve-hour day. It was therefore with a mixture of amazement, concern and excitement that Valerie discovered she was pregnant in November. The flat we were renting was too small for a baby, and Valerie was clearly going to have to give up her job.

Uncle Robert came to the party again, promising to lend us £750 interest-free as a deposit to buy a house. (Robert later converted the loan into a gift and gave the same amount to each of his other nephews and nieces, a further measure of his great generosity.) It was a huge leg-up just when it was needed most.

In early 1961, weekends were spent borrowing Dick's car and looking at places in the southern suburbs of London, and we decided on 69 Pine Ridge, Carshalton Beeches, which we purchased for £3,750 and moved into in April. It was a semi-detached house with three bedrooms, two smallish living rooms and a garden. We figured it would be plenty big enough for bringing up the baby.

Since she was booked in at Hastings Maternity Hospital, Valerie went back down to Bexhill and stayed with Dick and Dorrie from the beginning of July for the last stage of her pregnancy. On the third Saturday she was away I received a phone call at about six p.m. to say that a baby girl had arrived and she and Valerie were doing fine. Rather reluctantly I turned off *The Lone Ranger* and went to see them.

Two years later our second offspring arrived, at the small maternity hospital in Carshalton. Jeremy Mark Wavell joined his sister Juliet Claire as the newest member of the Hampton clan.

24. Reflections

SO it's 1962, I was twenty-five, I had a wife and one-year-old daughter, a semi-detached house on the outskirts of London, and a manageable mortgage.

I had lived through a world war – and survived a Public School! – as well as the decade of the fifties, when Great Britain was still recovering from the terrible toll of the wartime years. Now the nation was feeling a bit more prosperous and relaxed. In 1957, Prime Minister Harold Macmillan told us that we "had never had it so good", and for many of us this was true. Real earnings were on the rise and electrical and other household goods were readily available. The first independent television licences were granted to Associated Television (Midlands weekdays and London weekends), Associated-Rediffusion (London weekdays), Granada (Yorkshire and Lancashire weekdays) and Associated British Picture Corporation (Midlands, Yorkshire and Lancashire weekends), all of which gave the BBC a helluva shake-up – and provided me with a new employer.

The '50s had brought many changes. In music we progressed (I think) through the "strict tempo" of Victor Silvester and his Ballroom Orchestra to the "skiffle" of Lonnie Donegan and into the new sound of "trad" jazz. I became a huge fan of Humphrey Lyttelton as well as the bands of Acker Bilk, Chris Barber and Kenny Ball (known as the "3Bs"), all of whom played regularly during summer at the White Rock Pavilion in Hastings.

And then there was rock 'n' roll!

Bill Haley and His Comets got us up on the dance floor to *Rock Around the Clock* in 1955, followed by Elvis Presley, Johnny Cash, Carl Perkins and all those other influential American singers. In England we had home-grown performers who were making their own hits, Tommy Steele and Cliff Richard being two of the earliest.

Even Auntie BBC had pioneered a TV program featuring pop music: *Six-Five Special* debuted on my twentieth birthday, and although it only lasted for twelve months or so it gave rise to *Top of the Pops*, which ran for years, introduced a whole generation of young artists to a wider audience, and put their records on the charts.

In 1951, the first *Goon Show* was broadcast and it immediately snared a younger audience. I remember Dick and Dorrie sitting there listening to the radio and never once smiling. They didn't understand the wacky characters or get the crazy gags. I cracked up, and each show would be discussed endlessly at work the next day. *The Goon Show* was so different from earlier BBC comedies with its irreverence and unpredictability. One episode really put our home town on the map: *The Dreaded Batter Pudding Hurler of Bexhill.*

The Goons were, of course, the predecessors of brilliant new television formats. In 1962, a satirical show on Saturday nights introduced us to David (now Sir David) Frost and him to us. *That Was The Week That Was* became so popular that young people like us would only accept dinner invitations if the hosts promised to switch it on. There were no recording devices or catch-up replays available in those days.

Despite these significant changes and our emergence from post-war gloominess London in 1962 remained a pretty tame place, and out in the provinces most people continued to live relatively conservative lives. Then the Swinging Sixties went off like a bomb, and it was great to be at the epicentre of that cultural explosion which sent shockwaves all the way to Australia. Now it's time to go back there, to pick up the new direction my life and career took after I parted company with EMI.

SECTION FOUR: THE SWEETEST SOUNDS OF ALL

25. Going Steady

AS phone calls go, I have rarely taken one so pivotal to my whole life. It was from Brett Cottle, who had transferred some years earlier from APRA to its sister association AMCOS (of which more later) as the CEO and just been appointed CEO at APRA. He wanted to know if I'd be interested in being interviewed for the shortly-to-become vacant position as his deputy – officially the company secretary.

Interested, Brett? Try very! I was interviewed by Mike Perjanik, the chairman, and John Bromell, a board member, and I started on the first of September, 1990.

APRA was founded in 1926 on the UK model of the Performing Right Society (PRS). The name describes exactly what it does: it handles the performing right in music to which the composers, songwriters and publishers have a legal entitlement. In short, the Copyright Acts require a royalty to be paid any time a piece of music which is still "in copyright" is played, whether it be live, recorded or broadcast. Royalties also now apply to downloads and streaming provided by iTunes, Spotify and the like.

APRA's not-for-profit constitution provides for a board of twelve directors, six elected by the composer/songwriter members and six by the publishers. It is affiliated to the other national collecting societies through CISAC (the Confederation Internationale des Sociétés d'Auteurs et Compositeurs), the worldwide governing and policy-making organisation for all types of creators. This ensures that royalties received in, say, the USA for the performance of a song written by an Australian are funnelled back to APRA for distribution to the owners/holders of the copyright.

When I joined it, APRA was receiving royalties of around fifty million dollars a year and had about a hundred staff. It has grown substantially since then.

I enjoyed working with the board and particularly the writer members. At the time of my arrival they still included Dorothy Dodd, Glenn Shorrock and Ray Columbus (from my own days as a director), plus Mike Perjanik, a very successful writer for television, and the classical composer Richard Meale. They were joined shortly afterwards by Jenny Morris and Chris Neal, who was enjoying a growing reputation for his film music.

The job as company secretary became vacant because my predecessor had rather too close a relationship with the now retired CEO. I remembered her well from my time on the board and never found her the least bit helpful. Brett, who had been APRA's legal officer, made it conditional on his appointment that she be given early retirement. The directors were generous and she was probably pleased to leave.

My duties encompassed relationships with the directors, overseeing the membership services department, attending board and committee meetings, standing in for Brett when necessary, and all the other requirements of a company secretary from HR to administration. There was always plenty to do, and during my first year, when the office building which APRA owned was redesigned and refurbished floor-by-floor, I was very much in charge.

I had a great helper, my PA Kathryn Williams, of whom I cannot speak too highly. She saw me through fourteen years of considerable change, always with a smile. The fact that we both loved the TV series *Blackadder* helped and we nicknamed many of our colleagues after its characters. When Brett saw an episode and realised he was Baldrick he wasn't thrilled. "You bastards!" he said to us the next morning.

Mitchell Allen was the project manager for that first refurb, dealing with architects and designers. Later on he managed the refurbishment and relocation when APRA bought a bigger building in St Leonards to house increasing staff numbers.

Mitchell was enormously talented in office design but inexperienced in project management – we made a perfect match.

APRA afforded me another greatly appreciated benefit. Lucy was now twenty and decided to sample life in Australia. She stayed for nearly a year and I managed to smuggle her into a part-time secretarial job at APRA where she became my eyes and ears for much that was going on around her.

*   *   *

As Brett's 2-IC, I got the chance to go to a couple of biennial CISAC World Congresses. We were encouraged to take wives or partners, so in 1992 Jean and I headed for a little-known town in the south of Holland where the Continental leaders had just signed the agreement that propelled the political and economic integration of the European Union: the Maastricht Treaty.

I enjoyed meeting the delegates at Maastricht – who came from around sixty countries – and seeing them in action, but the social interaction was dull and the "entertainment" consisted of a performance by the Royal Dutch Ballet. Jean and many others said it was excellent, but I endured it in silence.

Thanks to Brett, we were staying at a popular heritage hotel in the centre of Maastricht built over the ruins of a Roman fort. The basement had been excavated, artefacts two thousand years old discovered, and history just oozed out of the ambience.

Around town the annual jazz festival was taking place, and in the evenings every bar and café offered a choice of top-class live combos. It made up for the boring ballet, in my book.

Two years later we attended an altogether different event in Washington DC. From the opening ceremony where delegates were treated to a fanfare specially composed by Morton Gould (who was a co-chairman of ASCAP, one of the American equivalents of APRA) and played by a band of US Marines until the close of proceedings, it was a sheer spectacular: America at its best and most showy. During the daily conference sessions wives and partners were taken around the tourist spots of the city and to private homes of the rich and famous. Jean told us that one property had a garden wall painted by Marc Chagall, who did it as a "thank you" to his dinner hosts. Must have been some dinner party.

The conference sessions were fairly routine and spent listening in the main to the problems some countries were having in getting their rights recognised; many of the Asian societies, for instance, had problems for decades. Brett was on a few panels and I was impressed by the respect given to him by his peers, many of whom were considerably older. He clearly knew his stuff and was one of the few with a comprehensive legal background. It came as no surprise that within a few years he was the chairman of CISAC, although he did tell me this was in part due to the fact that the Americans would not accept the British candidate and vice versa.

Two events stand out like beacons in my recollection of that conference. First, the lunch for fifty people, where the guest of honour and speaker was a charming Senator Edward Kennedy and a young choir conducted by Marvin Hamlisch, composer of *A Chorus Line*, entertained us singing his songs. And then the jaw-dropping entertainment our hosts programmed on the last night.

Nearly a thousand guests including delegates and their partners and celebrities gathered for dinner at the Institute of Architects, which is located in a building where the extraordinary interior features high ornate walls that imitate the exterior of a classical temple. Tables of eleven were uniformly set in gold and black, each hosted by a member of Congress or the Senate. We were greeted by an African-American congresswoman from Chicago, a delightful dinner companion who sat next to me.

After the main courses we were escorted onto buses and taken through driving rain to the White House. On the way our invitations and passports were checked by FBI agents – one guest was detained for investigation – and on arrival at 1600 Pennsylvania Avenue we were met by students with umbrellas who whisked us into a side entrance. Every few yards a hefty and well-armed Marine stood guard as we walked through the lower ground floor and out into a huge marquee erected on the immaculate lawn where a small aircraft had recently crashed, requiring the surface to be levelled and returfed – since when it had rained incessantly. The hordes of guests, staff and security agents tramping across the grass turned the lawn into a quagmire. I watched women digging in the mud to retrieve their shoes.

When everyone was assembled we were officially greeted from the stage – by none other than President Bill Clinton, who was absolutely charming, just as he came across on TV. After the presidential welcome waiters brought out dessert, coffee and wine – then the show began. *And what a show!* The Pointer Sisters, Lyle Lovett, Booker T and the MGs, Michael Bolton, a concert of stellar performances to end to an unforgettable four-day congress . . . and Jean still has the commemorative program.

*   *   *

Brett and I were keen to acquiesce when the board asked us to reformat the annual APRA Awards. Kathryn and I were put in charge of the 1991 event, which is how I met Peter Rix.

"Rixie" had been putting on shows and events since he was a teenager and he organised the staging and production. In those days the evening comprised drinks and a black-tie dinner followed by the awards ceremony presided over by a celebrity. We homed in on Jonathan Biggins, the comedian and satirist, as our regular MC. Jonathan went on to become even better known when he started to direct the annual *Wharf Revue* in 2000.

The APRA Awards were principally designed to honour Australian music, although in deference to our USA and UK counterparts – and to encourage some of their top brass to come to Sydney – we always had an award for "Most Performed Foreign Work".

In 1991, there were ten award categories culminating in "Song of the Year" – Yothu Yindi's *Treaty*. Their performance on the night was doubly memorable because this was the first APRA Award to go to indigenous songwriters.

We staged our ceremonies along similar lines at the Regent Hotel until 2000, each time catering for about five hundred guests and showcasing award nominees in live performances. As APRA's seventy-fifth anniversary was coming up in 2001 the directors wanted something different, so we hatched a plan to include more guests, more live performances – and cap the milestone with a list of the thirty greatest Australian songs, voted by a panel of one hundred music personalities and compiled in great secrecy by (you've guessed it!) Kathryn and myself. We went to extraordinary lengths to restrict details of the Top 10 filtered from the thirty to the "must-knows", like Rixie and the performers who agreed to play those songs on the night.

The "Ten Best and Significant Australian Songs of the Past 75 Years" were announced as the APRA Award winners were named, and the top song was *Friday on my Mind* by The Easybeats. You Am I played it, with Harry Vanda, the co-writer with George Young, guesting on guitar. The runner-up was *Eagle Rock*, performed by the songwriter, Ross Wilson, and his band, Daddy Cool. These two songs dated back to 1966 and 1971 and obviously appealed strongly to the voters, most of whom would have been in their teens or twenties when the records were released. At number three was *Beds Are Burning* by Midnight Oil. We showed a video clip of this powerful song, introduced by Senator Aden Ridgeway as an indigenous spokesperson on reconciliation, and he was very well received.

One song from the 1950s made the Top 10: *A Pub With No Beer* (at five), a chart-topper in '57. This quintessential Aussie ballad written by Gordon Parsons was of course performed on the night by Slim Dusty. The only other pre-sixties song in the Top 30 was *Along The Road To Gundagai* written by Jack O'Hagan in 1922. If my arithmetic is correct, that date was just outside the seventy-five-year criteria. But perhaps at the time we thought this folk classic simply had to be included.

We held that APRA anniversary on the twenty-eighth of May, 2001, at Royal Randwick Racecourse, one of the few Sydney venues at the time that could cater for a thousand guests – twice as many as we had ever invited previously. And it would have gone off without a hitch . . . if the weather had been fine. It was a shocker. It rained throughout the evening and the ladies' toilets were on the far side of a large courtyard. We had to organise a fleet of cars to ferry the girls back and forth to the loo! That was the only dampener on what must rank as one of the best nights in APRA's history. The performances and the archival video material we screened were greatly applauded. And the board members went home happy.

The next year we recast the APRA Awards, splitting them into three separate events because the current format did not give due recognition to genres of music outside the popular mainstream. Two new ceremonies were inaugurated: the Screen Music Awards and the Classical Music Awards.

We presented the Screen Music Awards in conjunction with the Australian Guild of Screen Composers at the Hordern Pavilion, where a superb orchestra played selections from the nominations.

The Classical Music Awards (subsequently renamed the Art Music Awards) were hived off to the main hall of the Sydney Conservatorium. This was an event especially enjoyed by the composers and their families. In 2002, we honoured Robert Hughes who had been an APRA board member and was most supportive of me back in the early '80s.

These two new events were a big step forward in widening our appreciation for the diversity of Australian music. And for me, the introduction to so many more songwriters and composers was a reward in itself.

After helping to co-ordinate the APRA Awards for thirteen years it was time to take a back seat and I began handing over my active role to Sally Howland. I had enjoyed being the executive producer.

*   *   *

One other Sydney-based arts event should be mentioned: the Sydney International Piano Competition which began in 1977. By the 1990s it had become a highly acclaimed cultural contest held every four years which culminated in the finals at the Opera House.

Sam Miller, an Old Eastbournian who was a director of the SIPC, invited Jean and I to the finals in 1992. One thing missing from the competition was recognition of serious or classical music composed by Australians, and over the next few years, as Sam introduced me to his fellow directors including the chairman, the late Warren Thompson, we discussed ways to remedy that. For the 1996 competition I put a proposal to the APRA board to offer a $10,000 prize for the best performance of a piece of Australian music, as well as organising public workshops hosted by Australian composers.

The APRA directors agreed. We had a great response from the competitors and attracted composers such as Peter Sculthorpe, Carl Vine, Ross Edwards and Nigel Westlake to the workshops. The overall winner of the piano competition and the cash prize that year was Sergei Tarasov – and APRA had more runs on the board in its mission to promote all types of Australian music.

*   *   *

AMCOS, the Australian Mechanical Copyright Owners Society, is the sister organisation to APRA. It collects the "mechanical" royalties (i.e. the royalty paid on the reproduction of music onto a CD or vinyl LP) which arise when music still in copyright is recorded and sold if the company making the recording does not have an agreement with the composer's publisher to make payments direct.

In those days the major record companies all had agreements with the major publishers, but there were several independents making different types of records – TV compilations for example, like Telmak's – and they accounted to AMCOS, which also had the important role of carrying out audits on behalf of the music publishers, as well as receiving royalties from overseas.

The merger of the APRA and AMCOS administrative functions was long overdue when Brett and I put forward the proposal to both boards in the mid-nineties. The savings in overheads should have been enough to convince even the self-protective directors of AMCOS.

When downloading started neither the songwriter nor the artist received any remuneration, and it was very unclear whether legislation could stop or regulate it. This is where CISAC came in, and within a few years laws were enacted and agreements reached worldwide between legitimate providers like iTunes and the music industry. But downloading was still a huge threat to societies like AMCOS, who were collecting the mechanical royalties not being paid directly by the record producers to the publishers.

Perhaps perversely – in the sense that we did not foresee this outcome – the revenue now derived from legitimate downloading and streaming provides the most substantial part of APRA/AMCOS income while illegitimate downloading has become less widespread.

*   *   *

After the 1994 CISAC conference Brett recruited Scot Morris to be the international director, so I didn't get to go to any more of those great parties like the one they put on at the White House, although I was still doing quite a bit of travel in Australia and overseas.

Since I was nominally overseeing the APRA membership department I chaired members' meetings in the other state capitals for a while. These were usually quite entertaining as I would have with me a publisher and a writer to answer questions, one of which I remember clearly.

We were in Perth with a good turnout, over sixty members. A young woman at the back of the room put up her hand and said: "I've been writing music in Sydney for some time but found the going hard, so I moved to Perth for some extra head space. Was that good?" The publisher on the panel said: "You moved here from Sydney?" He sounded incredulous. "You should always head for *bigger* markets, not smaller ones. Go to London."

You can imagine how that went down with the locals, but most of them knew he was right.

New Zealand was on my itinerary again and when our GM, a lawyer, resigned, Brett Cottle appointed a new one right out of the music industry: Mike Chunn, who had been the bass player for Split Enz from their start in 1972 until 1977. Mike knew everyone involved in music in the Shaky Isles and our membership grew on his watch.

I visited New Zealand regularly and got to know Mike and his lovely family really well. They invited Jean and I to stay one summer weekend at their house up on the north-west coast where the sand is black from volcanic ash . . . and HOT! By the way, *The Piano* was filmed near there.

On another occasion when quite a few directors and senior staff from Australia were attending the APRA NZ Silver Scrolls, their annual awards, we were met at the venue by a traditional Maori welcoming party with whom we rubbed noses. Their chief sang. Then they told us that our chief had to sing. We thought our chief was going to pass out. But Eric McCusker stepped forward, did a beautiful, unaccompanied rendering of *Come Said The Boy,* and Brett didn't need the smelling salts.

Fiji was also on my itinerary and I went there quite frequently to talk to writers and discuss copyright protection issues with the government. One year I presented some of the prizes at the Fiji Music Awards. At the dinner I was seated between the Attorney-General, a great conversationalist, and his wife, both well built people. Then it was dance time, and boy, could she dance!

*   *   *

My fourteen years with APRA/AMCOS were generally enjoyable. I rekindled many old relationships and forged many new ones in the music industry and other creative fields. One example of the latter was my nomination for the board of the Audio-Visual Copyright Society.

AVCS was incorporated in 1989 to license film and television programs for use in schools. My knowledge of APRA was useful to AVCS and there was another big benefit: Jean was hired as office manager, and the job description included accounting. She quickly learned MYOB and stayed at AVCS for nearly ten years.

But by 2004 I'd had enough and suggested that Dean Ormston take over my role as company secretary. The board gave me a great send-off dinner where I was presented with a silkscreen print of *The Black Cat*, a Charles Blackman painting I loved. People said some complimentary things about me, and the writer/director Richard Meale commented that I was the first bean-counter he'd ever met who had read Proust. Looking around the room all I could see was "Who the fuck is Proust?" on most of the faces.

I was also given the opportunity of reforming AMPAL, the Australasian Music Publishers' Association, on a part-time basis and working from home. After AMCOS had effectively merged with APRA the music publishers felt that they had no separate voice. They were happy to have APRA/AMCOS pay me a modest salary to look after their interests and organise get-togethers. I did this for a further three years, up to my seventieth birthday, and then it was "goodbye!"

I have the fondest memories of my involvement with APRA/AMCOS, first as a director and then as an executive. I rediscovered that I rather liked being a number two (perhaps I have a bit of Iago in me) and it was a pleasure to work with and for someone like Brett, who let me get on with the things I was good at. To the other executives – Andy, Sally, Gus, Scot, Dean, Chris, Milly, Michelle (and I hope I haven't missed anyone), plus of course Kathryn and Jennifer Reynolds who held the fort when Brett and I were away – thank you one and all.

26. Giving

IN 1976, the music industry worldwide was doing very well and nowhere was doing better than London. Sales of vinyl and cassettes were still increasing, and promoters were seeking ever larger concert spaces to accommodate ever bigger audiences. It was time for some new adventures.

In this vein, musicians and managers across the industry in the United Kingdom formed the Silver Clef, which started off as a lunch club and became a major charity. It presented its first award for outstanding achievement in music to The Who. Silver Clef's second objective was to raise money for children's charities, of which Nordoff-Robbins Music Therapy was the first and continues to be a major beneficiary.

Two expat Australian music publishers who were aware of the Silver Clef decided to adopt the idea for Sydney, and so in 1979 the Golden Stave was born and the first funds were raised. Throughout the 1980s, what became known as "the longest lunch of the year" thrived, earning increasing amounts from annual ticket sales and an auction, but by 1990 the organising committee felt that the Stave needed greater flexibility and transparency, and it was decided to set up a trust called the Golden Stave Foundation. Its objectives would be to provide funds to tax-deductible gift recipients whose aims were to help people, children in particular, with physical, mental and emotional problems.

I first became involved at the 1988 lunch when I was asked to supervise the money collected from the raffles, auctions and donations, which I did in a draughty corridor at the back of the Four Seasons Hotel, assisted by a great bunch of wheelchair-bound men from Paraquad, for whom we were fundraising. In 1990, I was asked by the new trustees, of whom Barry Chapman was the chairman, to sort out the trust deed and get the endorsement of the Charities Commission which would lead to the necessary exemptions from tax. I was then appointed secretary to the trust, responsible for the accounting records and preparation of financial statements. Jean was by now familiar with MYOB and she kept the books for the next ten years. At each event Ron Welsh and Tim Denny from APRA helped me to collect and count the money raised before a Brinks armoured van arrived to pick it up.

During that decade support for the Golden Stave and its income grew, but each year the net amount distributable was limited to between three hundred and four hundred thousand dollars because we could only cater for about five hundred people at the fundraiser. So in 1998 we moved it to the Sydney Entertainment Centre, wined and dined one thousand guests – and raised and distributed five hundred and fifty-five thousand dollars. For several years afterwards the event continued to grow and the funds kept pouring in, but more recently, no doubt coinciding with the contraction of the traditional music industry, the proceeds from the lunch have greatly diminished.

I left the Golden Stave around the year 2000, but it had been a great experience – and it led me on to Nordoff-Robbins Music Therapy.

*   *   *

I got another of those life-changing phone calls. This time from Peter Hebbes, one of the founders of the Golden Stave. He knew that in London the Silver Clef gave most of its funds to Nordoff-Robbins, which had built a centre for providing creative music therapy, and the word "creative" was the key. Until Paul Nordoff and Clive Robbins collaborated, most music therapy was passive (like just listening to music) or unstructured. Paul, a celebrated American composer and pianist, and Clive, an English child psychologist, introduced a radically different and comprehensive form of therapy. It involved initial assessments of people's specific physical, intellectual and emotional problems and needs, leading to the composition of customised music pieces to encourage their participation in therapy sessions. The Nordoff-Robbins philosophy pioneered the use of improvisational music techniques to enable everyone being treated to reach their full potential.

I heard Paul play and talk about music improvisation at that 1976 lunch in London. He died the following year, but I got to know Clive well because he came to Sydney several times, and on one occasion stayed with us at Wentworth Falls.

Clive was a captivating speaker at a lectern or around a dinner table: authoritative but not didactic, with a great sense of self-deprecatory humour. His visits were always of great benefit to us, enthusing his audience and gathering support.

My involvement accelerated when Peter Hebbes contacted me after attending a meeting of people who were trying to get Nordoff-Robbins on the map in Australia. He was horrified by what he heard about their promotional and financial management and asked me to get involved.

The instigator within this group was Enid Rowe, who had trained in London as a music therapist and brought the Nordoff-Robbins concept to Australia in the 1970s. She established a clinical practice at a Steiner school for the disabled in a semi-rural area north of Sydney. In 1993, Enid asked Robin Howat, who also trained at the Nordoff-Robbins centre in London, to come to Australia to set up a teaching course, and he arrived with his wife, Jane, and their two young children.

By 1996, when Peter called me, everything was badly off the rails. Although Enid had a ready-made clientele she was only making a small income. And while the Steiner school was also Robin's teaching base, its location didn't attract many students. Nor did their course for a Diploma in Music Therapy lead to any qualification acceptable to the Australian Music Therapy Association (AMTA) in Melbourne.

I was invited to an emergency meeting of the Nordoff-Robbins committee which was made up of elderly ladies and one elderly gent. I was nearly sixty, but these people were old! The only exception was Judith Rutherford, who was enormously supportive then and later. No accounts were available, but it was admitted that funds to support Robin were low and no fundraising activities were planned. I arranged to visit the treasurer's home to look at the books – and found a cash book and a petty cash book.

"Why are these written up in pencil?" I asked.

"In case I have to rub them out," was the old lady treasurer's reply.

I arranged to take over the cash books, transfer the current year's transactions onto MYOB, and prepare a set of accounts. Fortunately the treasurer had kept bank statements.

What I found was alarming: only sufficient funds on hand to pay Robin for another month. I was deputed to meet him and break the bad news. He was made redundant with the promise that, if we could get things organised, we would keep in touch. He was surprisingly calm and said he could work from home and build up his own client base for therapy. Fortunately Jane Howat had found employment as a teacher.

We were then asked by the committee to put forward suggestions for a reorganisation of their affairs. It took four years of hard work by quite a few people to get Nordoff-Robbins properly established in Australia.

*   *   *

I needed advice on the best way to go forward and contacted Peter Townsend, who was the husband of Margaret, my PA at EMI. Peter was a solicitor and we had kept in touch. I was always impressed with his business-like outlook and he was aware of the Golden Stave.

Peter came up trumps and offered to produce – gratis – a business plan for Nordoff-Robbins in Australia. It proposed:

- That Nordoff-Robbins Music Therapy Australia (NRMTA) be incorporated as a not-for-profit legal entity, preferably a limited company so that it could legitimately trade but be non-taxable.

- That a new board be elected with members who could give wide access to the music industry for fundraising purposes.
- That a course in music therapy be designed and delivered in partnership with a university which could grant a degree acceptable to the AMTA.
- That a clinical centre be established to attract other qualified music therapists.

The first two points were easily addressed and NRMTA Limited was incorporated in 1997, with a board comprised of Judith Rutherford as chair, myself as treasurer/company secretary, Peter Hebbes and Enid Rowe. Naomi Hadfield and Robin Howat were soon invited to join. Most of the old ladies were too, but they were all glad to lose their responsibility.

The next priority was to find a university interested in starting up a training course. Robin and I had meetings with the head of every music department in Sydney and considered Melbourne too, without success. Some academics were interested but not convinced that enough students could be enrolled to make the course viable, and others were disinterested in any form of improvisational music.

And then we got a big break, entering the orbit of Professor Michael Atherton, Head of the Music Department at the University of Western Sydney (now Western Sydney University), who had heard about us. Michael had studied music therapy – amongst many things he is also an expert on indigenous musical instruments – and soon he and Robin were putting together a plan for a Graduate Diploma in Music Therapy which was eventually accepted by his Vice-Chancellor.

At the same time we discovered that UWS was encouraging third parties to put new projects into its Kingswood campus. We set out on the lengthy process of agreeing to terms for a twenty-year lease on a parcel of land to build a centre housing the music therapy practice and the diploma course. Our friend and neighbour in Wentworth Falls, Peter Warth, offered to draw up the architectural plans gratis in consultation with Robin, and when that was finished and costed out, all we had to do was find the money.

The NRMTA directors debated our development proposal: whether it was good commercial practice to expend a considerable amount of money erecting a building on land under a lease that might not be offered again to NRMTA when it expired. Then they agreed unanimously that it was the best way of achieving our objectives, approved our building proposal subject to raising the funds, and also agreed to offer the management of the centre to Robin Howat.

Robin closely followed in Clive Robbins' footsteps in his approach to music therapy and his ability to hold an audience. Where he differed was in his understanding that for a Nordoff-Robbins centre to flourish in Australia, economically and politically, it had to offer its services to the broader community. Clive had very few private clients, and required substantial support to underwrite his own practice. We could not afford to operate that way – every fundraising dollar had to go towards the functioning of the centre itself.

The design of the dual-purpose centre was especially important: incorporating all of the uses each room could be put to and the requirements for therapy sessions, teaching, meetings and interviews, plus administration and instrument storage. Peter came up with a design for a boomerang-shaped, single-level structure without stairs to make it accessible for disabled people. The entrance and reception area were in the middle, and behind that a room for teaching, spacious enough for meetings and small performances too. There were two music therapy rooms, each with a piano and space for the client, two therapists and other instruments, and windows placed well above head height to allow in light and keep out distractions. These therapy rooms also had their own "viewing" room attached, allowing parents, teachers or people to whom we were demonstrating our approach to music therapy to watch a session through one-way glass and listen in via hidden microphones without the client knowing anyone was there (provided the therapist was in agreement). We used the viewing rooms very effectively to encourage several of our ambassadors to help us.

Raising the money and building the centre took three years. We needed six hundred and fifty thousand dollars for the building, fitout and equipment, and this was where our connections with the Golden Stave, the music industry and various contractors and suppliers paid off. We leaned on all of them without mercy.

The Stave virtually guaranteed to let us have four hundred and fifty thousand dollars over the next three years, and then we contacted building contractors I had got to know through APRA, as well as suppliers of office furniture and equipment and sympathetic retailers of musical instruments, to ramp things up.

We held our first fundraising event in March 1998, the annual music trivia night at North Sydney Leagues Club – and twenty years later it was still going strong. The evening consisted of a buffet dinner followed by the quiz. Jean and I used to put the questions together, and we always secured a celebrity host. Our first was that rock music brain, Glenn A. Baker.

Teams of eight sat at separate tables, and from the outset the trivia quiz engendered huge competition between rival record companies. It raised an impressive amount, about twenty thousand dollars every time, and has proven to be a terrific way of getting the music business – indeed the whole entertainment industry – together once a year to remind them about the extraordinary work Nordoff-Robbins is doing with the wonder of music.

*   *   *

Michael Atherton did more than help to get us off the ground. He provided an introduction to someone who would become an important high-profile supporter of Nordoff-Robbins and also a great friend: Dr Marie Bashir, who had worked with Michael and was now the Governor of NSW. She readily agreed to be our Patron.

Which brings me to the Great Opening.

The building was finished, the graduate diploma was into its third year, therapists and administrative staff were hired and trained, and everything was in place. Invitations went out to sponsors, supporters and all the VIPs we could think of, asking them to join us and the State Governor on the first of November, 2001. More than one hundred guests were there to see Her Excellency officially open the Nordoff-Robbins Music Therapy Centre – what was and still is the largest custom-built music therapy centre in the southern hemisphere.

A dream realised.

27. And Receiving

NRMTA Limited now had a centre and a small but growing number of clients. From the beginning, Robin insisted that no one deserving who could be helped would be turned away if they could not afford our fees. In those days music therapy was not recognised by the health authorities as a reimbursable cost. Indeed, many in the medical profession were vocally opposed to music and other therapies that could not provide "cures".

As many of our clients could only pay part fees I remember that in the first year our gross profit yielded only twenty-seven per cent of total operating costs. The remainder had to be found by fundraising.

Therefore another person joined the staff: Nicci Gow, who was tasked with submitting applications for funding to charitable trusts and foundations, as well as helping to organise the mushrooming number of fundraising events and activities to raise awareness of our activities.

Over the years our fundraisers took many forms. Peter Sculthorpe once had a catered evening at his house in Paddington where he told a small but select number of guests what he understood about the use of music for therapeutic purposes. It was a huge success, and as I recall we managed to recruit some outstanding new members to the board that night, including Simon Thorp and Cameron Slapp, both partners at KPMG. Simon continues now as chairman and Cameron as treasurer, so we owe a great debt of gratitude to the late and delightful Peter Sculthorpe.

Jenny Morris, who was on the APRA board and now chairs it, became an important part of the fundraising team. Between us, and with lots of help from Peter Hebbes and Barry Chapman in particular, we organised several evenings of "Jenny Morris at The

Basement", the club famous (and now closed) in Sydney for jazz. Not only would Jenny sing, she also compered the evenings which included memorable appearances by Glenn Shorrock and Jimmy Barnes, among others.

So many famous people from the world of music performed for our fundraisers or became ambassadors and appeared at other events, such as open days at the centre. They included Col Joye, Joy McKean, Richard Clapton and many more. They knew what music could do for you, even if the medical profession didn't.

And then in 2006, Jenny Morris and Peter McLaughlin came up with "The Art of Music".

The basic idea had been used many times: ask artists to give you a painting and then auction it. Their twist was to ask artists to paint a visualisation of one of their favourite Australian songs. We also asked if they were prepared to give NRMTA all proceeds of the sale or whether they would donate up to seventy-five per cent. Most were very generous.

For that first auction we had paintings donated by Ben Quilty, Nicholas Harding, Reg Mombassa, Wendy Sharpe – an embarrassingly large number rolled in. Our auctioneer from Christie's, well versed in art, was taken aback. He said he did not have the time to sell more than ten and proceeded to choose the ones he thought were the best. We put the others into a secondary "silent" auction and some of the artists not chosen for the main show were none too pleased. Another important lesson.

Peter McLaughlin was a senior executive at Qantas who had dealings with big corporate entities for sponsorship, chiefly the Margaret River vineyards, and he sourced the wine for us. But even more exciting were those who gave their names to our advertising and took tables: they included our main sponsor, STELLAR, as well as Qantas, Macquarie Bank and Westfield. Between us we also got sponsorship from NAB and Warner Music. For a first event it was a huge lineup.

Through Peter we met Edmund Capon, head of the Art Gallery of New South Wales, and his assistant Leith Douglas, who became our main contact when Edmund agreed to let us hold the event in the Grand Hall of the Gallery. Another coup!

The first Art of Music auction on the sixth of October, 2006, was a sellout.

The evening began with drinks and the viewing of all the paintings, twenty-odd, as well as the chance to meet the artists. Dinner was served at tables of ten, followed by brief speeches of welcome and the entertainment. This was a brilliant mixture organised by Jenny: first the Sydney Children's Choir, for whom we had erected a stage to sing Nick Cave's *The Ship Song*; and then the highlight, Iva Davies singing *Great Southern Land*. Iva was joined for an impromptu and unrehearsed encore by our other good friend and star, Jimmy Barnes. I think all those who had bought sponsorships or tickets felt it was money well spent.

Then it was auction time. I had given the auctioneer a list of the big names in the audience and their tables so he could point them out and rev them up for bidding. What a strategy! It worked a treat and all the paintings were sold, most at prices well above their market value. We owed a big debt of thanks to the man from Christie's who made the auction such a success.

Next morning was tidying-up time, getting the artworks back to Essential Art Services who kindly looked after them until they could be delivered to their new owners, and recovering the unopened wine for another occasion. When we totted up the takings, we had netted a whopping three hundred thousand dollars.

The Art of Music was the most successful fundraiser in Sydney in 2006 and it has since been held every two years. To date it has raised well over two million dollars for the Nordoff-Robbins Music Therapy Centre.

*   *   *

The development and training of music therapists has always been a major goal for NRMTA. But after the centre opened in 2001, Robin Howat told us he couldn't handle the teaching as well as his own caseload of clients.

Dr Alan Lem was hired to take over management of the graduate diploma course. Alan is Polish by birth, a brilliant lutenist and an enjoyable man to spend time with. We used to invite him to private parties and he'd bring his guitar or lute to entertain our guests, sometimes by inviting audience participation, creating a very lively session.

During Alan's time the course was upgraded to a Masters in Creative Music Therapy, an advance that attracted more students and enhanced the status of our graduates.

*   *   *

We had been told by our English colleagues that the London Centre was becoming more involved in "community music", but Robin and Alan were initially resistant to this concept.

Nevertheless, we tried to make our services available to a wide range of people with disabilities. I asked a therapist to visit one of the Paraquad houses for which the Golden Stave had raised money for purchase and renovation several years earlier and talk to the residents. The therapist came back with a negative response.

By chance my old friend Max Bosotti, the director of Paraquad, invited me over a few months later to meet a mutual friend.

"Why don't your people want to come to us for music therapy?" I asked him.

"They don't want therapy," he replied. "They know they're disabled and they know they're not going to get better. So no therapy, but they would love to make music."

A busload of paraplegic and quadriplegic men plus their wheelchairs and helpers then began to arrive at the centre one day a week to "make music" together with the staff. Everyone enjoyed it and the word "therapy" was never mentioned. It's a happy memory that reminds us of the undeniable power and value of community music.

Shortly before Jean and I left NRMTA there was a dinner party in Penrith which a hundred-odd people attended. The highlight was the performance by five men from Paraquad plus two friends from the centre. One of the men could just beat time on a cymbal with a brush, others not so disabled kept time on drums and guitars, and one helped Iani Sujono, one of our therapists, pick out a simple melody on the piano. It was a rewarding experience for those making the music and their audience.

During our association with NRMTA from its inception in 1997 to 2011 we met so many gifted musicians and dedicated therapists that it would be impossible to remember them all. But some who stand out include Eudora Lowe, one of our first recruits, as well as Iani and Rob Devlin, both brilliant therapists who also have complementary business skills. It is satisfying to know that they have combined their talents to set up their own increasingly successful centre called Sound Expression.

*   *   *

Medicare's recognition of music therapy as one of various programs for life enhancement, therefore qualifying for partial fee relief, has been hugely welcomed by NRMTA and the whole profession. It has taken a huge load off the fundraising imperative, although that remains a critical part of achieving the Nordoff-Robbins Centre's goals. The Medicare breakthrough didn't happen while I was there, but I like to believe that all those visits to Canberra played a small part.

Two other major factors have, I think, been instrumental in expansion of the centre's activities. The first was the recruitment of a professional board which includes the KPMG partners I've mentioned as well as prominent leaders from business and the music industry. These include Chris Gardoll whom I've known since he was the KPMG partner responsible for the APRA audit in 1992, Les Gock, a successful businessman and an outstanding lead guitarist, Gus Jansen and Milly Petriella from APRA, and Alan Travers.

Alan's contribution has been notably enormous. When we met he was about to retire as the General Manager of Penrith City Council. He introduced us to influential people in the area, which includes Kingswood where the centre is located.

One of those important contacts was David Bradbury, the Mayor of Penrith who went on to become the Federal Member for the seat of Lindsay. David was in his late twenties at the time, married with a child he sometimes brought to the centre on open days. He never sought to take the limelight away from the therapists or their clients. He chatted easily to our guests and was always good value.

*   *   *

In 2011, we celebrated the tenth anniversary of the official opening and it was my last visit to Australia's only Nordoff-Robbins Centre. Working with all those wonderfully dedicated and inspirational people – the therapists, administrators, ambassadors, supporters, directors, and everyone who helped to set up the centre and ensure its success – has been one of the most treasured experiences of my life. All those involved gave a lot, and we all received much more in return.

On my leaving the board offered me the opportunity of becoming the Vice Patron and I was proud to accept. Just as I was to accept the Order of Australia Medal in the 2008 Australia Day Awards, a humbling and rewarding honour. The citation reads "for service to the community through a range of charitable organisations supporting people with physical, intellectual and emotional disabilities, and to the music industry". I felt like this award wasn't only mine – it belonged to everyone else too.

28. And Now . . .

IN late November 2011, Jean and I gave a dinner party for our friends in the Blue Mountains. While showing our guests out after another super night, I felt like I had walked into a wall: no energy, no breath. Less than a week later I was having a pacemaker implanted thanks to my cardiologist, Dr John England, and feeling alive again.

We had already decided to rent our house in Wentworth Falls (which we bought after moving from Blackheath) and spend at least one whole year in France, and so we left Sydney on the nineteenth of January, 2012, when I had fully recovered.

Eight years later, we're still in France. In 2019, we moved from our lovely old farmhouse in the south-west Tarn region into the apartment we bought in the nearest town, Castres, and have been renovating for the past few years. It's the ground floor of a very large house built towards the end of the 18th century, and has high ceilings (over three metres), a main living room of forty square metres, a south-facing terrace and a garden. We are very comfortable here and even our cat, Dumora, approves.

*   *   *

Yes, I've been looking back, but not too nostalgically. Jean and I lived and worked through nearly fifty years when the music industry threw off its baby clothes, became a wayward teenager, then reached adulthood and, perhaps finally, maturity.

In 1960, vinyl was just starting to replace shellac for record pressing and the big companies like EMI, Decca and RCA owned huge factories and distribution points in a score or more countries around the world.

In 1962, the cassette was invented and manufactured by Philips, yet only exploited as a device for dictation by secretaries in offices for the next six years. It wasn't until 1968 that cassettes were widely used for music recording. The explosion in motor vehicle sales, particularly in the United States, heralded the next big invention: eight-track and four-track tape, which was principally designed for in-car use. But neither format caught on in Europe where Philips were very clever at persuading car manufacturers to install cassette players in their new models.

Twenty years later, in 1982, the compact disc was released to a lukewarm reception from the music industry, due probably to the massive global investment the record companies had made in vinyl pressing and tape duplication plants – the last thing they wanted was another format. But as innovation has shown mankind down the ages, a revolutionary technological advance cannot be repulsed. The CD steadily gained ground due to its killer advantage over vinyl: the sheer quantity of music that could be stored on it.

In 1999, we had the biggest shock of all: Napster. The invention of this service provided music lovers with the opportunity of downloading their choice of pre-recorded music for free, and hundreds of thousands, mostly young people, jumped at it. The music industry in America was not slow in suing Napster for infringement of copyright, and after a protracted struggle the costs of the action forced Napster to close down.

Once again the people running the corporate music giants had been caught off guard, and they either did not notice – or ignored – what was happening outside their own world. But with the advent of iTunes, Spotify and other digital services, "downloading" and "streaming" have now become accepted and mostly legitimate parts of the worldwide music industry which produce large chunks of the total income flowing back to artists, songwriters, record companies and music publishers.

And what about the music? It's probably even more diverse than it was in the '60s, but Elton John is still around, playing to fans in packed stadiums who are paying more for a seat today than they would have dreamed about in his early days. In terms of spotting and promoting new artists, the ubiquitous television talent show predominates almost worldwide, and I'm sure it's harder to reach young people through radio play.

Certainly the *culture* (if one might take the liberty of calling it that!) of the industry has changed dramatically, with only three worldwide record companies left, all owned by multinationals with many other commercial interests.

I cannot imagine those cosy little gatherings of the 1960s with the Pye gang down at The Mason's Arms still taking place in 2020. Besides, the whole attitude of the workforce – at least the British workforce – has changed, along with so many facets of English life that used to be taken for granted. Far more married women are employed and far, far fewer employees are expecting that theirs is a job for life. But then I never thought mine was either.

A significant number of culture commentators and opinion makers like to call the period from the 1960s to the early 2000s "A Golden Age". It certainly was for the music industry and I was lucky to be a part of it. Jean and I have been extremely fortunate to work in a creative field where we met so many talented and interesting people, and we hope that occasionally our very different skillsets in some way complemented theirs.

If I've done too much name-dropping I do apologise, but let's be honest, we all enjoy being associated with the celebs. So here is one last fond reminiscence, from 1978.

I am invited to an intimate lunch in St John's Wood. The door is opened and I am greeted with, "May I take your hat and coat, sir?" by Ron Moody, who starred as Fagin both on stage in *Oliver!* the musical and in the film. Inside I find the composer Lionel Bart worshipping at the feet of Dame Vera Lynn. These people weren't just *celebs* they were *legends*. Great memories.

As for my own taste in tunes, these days I mostly go to classical music and jazz concerts. Although I have to admit that I still like to put on my Andy Williams *Christmas Album* as the festive season gets under way. (That's our little secret, okay?)

*   *   *

It may have been a golden age for the music industry and for me. We haven't had a cataclysmic war, many of us have enjoyed interesting and occasionally fruitful lives, but there have been downsides too. The overall prosperity of "the West" has not been fairly shared out and many families are worse off now than they were ten years ago. In my early twenties I could, with a bit of help, buy our first house within an easy commute of London. Today my oldest grand-daughter, who is twenty-seven, and her boyfriend, both earning very good money, can just afford to rent a small flat.

In the UK many of the reforms to healthcare, education, social benefits and welfare brought in after 1945 seem to be steadily deteriorating; "privatisation" is just an easy way of ensuring that nobody takes responsibility for anything. Those who do care are becoming ever more marginalised.

Corruption has always started with the "suits", and that becomes more and more evident each day with corporate chairmen and CEOs paying themselves fat bonuses and maintaining share prices with dividends from cash that should have been paid into pension funds. Corruption is like a stealthy but virulent infection: once you have accepted it in a colleague, or been prepared to overlook it, you are their prisoner.

When I make those sort of observations I realise how lucky, or perhaps discerning, we have been in our choice of friends. Jean and I still enjoy the companionship of many old acquaintances from our days in Australia, as well as the new ones – both French and expats – here in our new home. And our lovely family of course: we love spending time with you.

Have I learned anything? Two things perhaps. My early distrust of those in authority and my questioning of "experts" has proved correct more often than not. And I'm probably still making some of the same mistakes I did decades ago. BUT . . . I do now accept and, I hope, reciprocate the love offered to me. And I am still looking forward.

INDEX

TRANSFORMING LIVES THROUGH MUSIC

When Nordoff-Robbins Music Therapy Australia (NRMTA) began providing clinical programs over two decades ago, the perception of music therapy (and its benefit) was limited.

Today NRMTA is at the forefront of music therapy and widely regarded as exemplars in the field. Each week over 1300 people access the wide range of music therapies provided. Evidence-based therapies are provided to support people (from small children to adults over 100 years old) who get real benefit from the services.

These services include individual and group sessions available at NORO (the new name for NRMTA) clinics in Kingswood, Penrith, Glenbrook, Richmond and Annangrove. NORO partners with early learning centres, schools, day programs, hospitals, community support services and nursing homes to run outreach programs across the greater Sydney region.

For more information: www.noro.org.au or phone (02) 4736 0240.

For over 40 years The Golden Stave has been supported by the Australian music and entertainment industries and associated organisations.

The Golden Stave Foundation was formed as a not-for-profit trust fund for the purpose of providing money, property or benefits to funds, authorities or institutions, endorsed as deductible gift recipients, which contribute towards the relief of poverty, destitution, sickness, helplessness and misfortune amongst persons and particularly children suffering from physical, intellectual and emotional disabilities.

Each year The Golden Stave runs two charity events: the Golf Day and the infamous Golden Stave Lunch, which raise money for sick, underprivileged and handicapped children in NSW.

Since 1979, the foundation has raised over $15 million for more than 50 children's charities in NSW.

For more information: www.goldenstave.com.au. Or contact Larry Warren, General Manager on 0406 428 969 and larry@goldenstave.com.au.

SUPPORTACT
The heart & hand of Australian music

Support Act is Australia's charity delivering crisis relief services to artists, crew and music workers as a result of ill health, injury, a mental health problem, or some other crisis that impacts on their ability to work in music.

Assistance can take the form of paying the rent or the mortgage, buying a bed or wheelchair, and paying for car repairs or bills such as medical, dental, phone and electricity, or a credit card debt. Also, providing referrals to other support services, funding for funerals, and support for friends and family seeking to raise funds.

Support Act raises funds from the music industry and its supporters.

For more information: www.supportact.org.au or phone 1300 731 303.

Printed in Great Britain
by Amazon